LIFE LESSONS
HARRY POTTER TAUGHT ME

*Discover the Magic of Friendship, Family,
Courage and Love in Your Life*

Jill Kolongowski

Ulysses Press

Published in the United States by:
Ulysses Press
P.O. Box 3440
Berkeley, CA 94703
www.ulyssespress.com

ISBN: 978-1-61243-724-8
Library of Congress Control Number 2017938173

Printed in Canada by Marquis Book Printing
10 9 8 7 6 5 4 3 2 1

Acquisitions: Bridget Thoreson
Managing editor: Claire Chun
Editor: Shayna Keyles
Proofreader: Renee Rutledge
Front cover design: Justin Shirley
Cover photo: © Firma V/shutterstock.com
Interior design: what!design @ whatweb.com
Interior art © shutterstock.com: Lighting bolt, merion_merion; page 6, Martial Red; 12, 98, Semiletava Hanna; 23, Francois Poirier; 34, Jemastock; 43, DODOMO; 55, Janis Abolins; 65, Park Ji Sun; 73, newarta; 86, In-Finity; 105, Sudowoodo; 119, veronchick84; 125, Vector1st; 138, VectorSun; 146, agrino; 156, VectorShop

Distributed by Publishers Group West

For my family

CONTENTS

INTRODUCTION 1

LUMOS:
On Discovery, Wonder, and Cynicism 6

AGUAMENTI:
On Home, Food, Family, and Belonging. 12

PRIORI INCANTATEM:
On Connecting Generations 23

FIDELIUS:
On Betrayal and Loyalty 34

LEGILIMENS:
On Good People and Death Eaters 43

SPECIALIS REVELIO:
On Fate and Free Will 55

EVANESCO:
On Losing Our Heroes 65

RENNERVATE:
On Knowledge and Loss of Innocence 73

EXPECTO PATRONUM:
On Loneliness, Friendship, and Community 86

PROTEGO:
On Kindness 98

FLAGRATE:
On Prejudice and Respect 105

SONORUS:
On the Power of Words 119

IMPERIO:
On Breaking the Rules and
the Danger of Power 125

RIDDIKULUS:
On Laughter in Darkness 138

WINGARDIUM LEVIOSA:
On the Unbearable Rightness of Hermione. 146

PETRIFICUS TOTALUS:
On Bravery. 156

ACKNOWLEDGMENTS 166

ABOUT THE AUTHOR. 170

INTRODUCTION

I first picked up *Harry Potter and the Sorcerer's Stone* when I was 12 years old. By then, it was already too late for me to get my Hogwarts acceptance letter, but that didn't stop me from hoping. My younger sister and I shared the first three books and read and reread them until the glue in the binding started to wear and the pages started to detach from their spine. After *Prisoner of Azkaban*, we didn't want to share anymore. We wanted the pages to ourselves.

Every summer, my sister, my cousins, and I would bring our *Harry Potter* books to our family's lake house and read them while sprawled in the hammock or on the end of the wooden dock, our feet dangling in the cold water. We shushed each other to keep anyone from spoiling things and huddled together once we all reached the same place to discuss what happened. No matter what else was happening—someone going to high school, someone leaving it, someone's parents getting divorced—we all came together with Harry. I'd wanted my own secret, magical world my whole life, and here was one more beautiful and more real than anything I could have imagined.

I couldn't admit it then but I can now: The characters felt like friends to me. For 12-year-olds (Muggles and wizards and witches alike), the world starts to become strange. Your parents start to become real, flawed people, your friends become people you no longer recognize, and you don't want to look in the mirror most days. No matter how tangled things became in real life, I could always find my friends again, where I'd left them, at Hogwarts. And some kind of magic was always waiting for me.

I'm a literature professor. I have loved many books and forgotten many more. But I believe I'll never (truly, never) love reading a book as much as I loved reading *Harry Potter and the Deathly Hallows*. On that book-release Saturday, I had stupidly scheduled an important doctor's appointment. Breaking the speed limit by 20 miles per hour, I rushed to the appointment as if I could make time move faster if I wanted it to badly enough. The doctor wanted to chat while she pressed and prodded me, but I snapped at her. "I'm kind of in a hurry," I said, batting her hand away. When she was finished, I put my clothes back on like a slapstick comedian—buttons mismatched, fly undone, pant leg tucked into my shoe. I stuffed my socks in my pocket and ran out the door. In my car, my phone rang. It was my boyfriend at our apartment. "Guess what package came?" he said. I hung up the phone and sped through yellow lights. The end of everything was waiting.

For the last book, I had rules. I would stop reading only to eat and go to the bathroom. (Technically, I didn't break the rules.

I stayed put, spilling sandwich crumbs in the book's spine and sitting on the toilet to read for so long that my legs fell asleep.) I would not answer the phone. I would not stop until I was finished. To keep myself from reading too quickly and from peeking at the italicized spells and capital letters (which probably meant someone was dying), I used a piece of paper to cover the right-hand side of the page while I was on the left. Deliberately reading slowly, it took me 10 hours to read 759 pages. That's barely over a page each minute.

The first time I opened the last book, I traced the words on the inside front flap with my finger: "We now present the seventh and final installment in the epic tale of Harry Potter." J. K. Rowling had dedicated the book to her family, to her children who grew up with Harry, Ron, and Hermione like they were siblings. Then, she dedicated it to "you, if you have stuck with Harry until the very end." I had.

⚡⚡⚡

I've since returned to Harry many times. Every summer, I go home to Hogwarts and reread the series. Even after 20 years (*Harry Potter and the Philosopher's Stone* was published in 1997) the magic hasn't faded, and I'm not alone in continuing to turn to the series to visit old friends and familiar places as a source of guidance and comfort. We all continue to go home to Hogwarts.

The *Harry Potter* series continues to speak to readers, whether they just finished reading the books for the first time, they just finished a reread, or they're coming back again after many years away. (If you haven't read the books or seen the movies, consider this your spoiler alert.) As a child, you obsess over Florean Fortescue's ice cream, Hermione knowing how to do "*Wingardium Leviosa!*" better than anyone, and the beauty of the Burrow, and you enjoy hating Severus Snape and learning from Dumbledore with the trio. As an adult, you begin to understand the pressures and the struggles of the adults in the series, and over and over, learn lessons about loss and about love.

This book explores the many life lessons we can learn from Harry's story. From light (like the need to hold onto your ability to perceive wonder, the comfort of food, and the benefits of a good sense of humor) to dark (like the bravery of resisting oppression and the lack of a clear line between good and evil), this book will delve deep into all seven books and the characters within, and track how their stories map onto our lives while we keep waiting for our own Hogwarts letters to arrive.

While this book can never be exhaustive (I could keep writing this book forever, if I had the time), the lessons that appear again and again are about the friendships and loves that can save your life. Some chapters discuss how *Harry Potter* is about valuing the people around you and about creating your own best self from the sometimes awful, unfair, or ordinary cards you're dealt. Others describe how *Harry Potter* is about the biggest battle we'll all fight in our lives: the fight against evil and harm, whether that's on a global scale or if it's in the small battles of our everyday worlds. There is no chapter solely about love because every chapter is about love. And love in the inverse, as hatred, exists here, too; in Voldemort, and sometimes even in Harry. But everything comes back to love in some form or another—love of family, love of friends, love of yourself.

This year I turned to *Harry Potter* when, in the same month, a student of mine died, a mentor of mine died, and I began to worry about the future of the country. Though Harry didn't save my life or start a love story (though I've heard of Harry doing both of those very things), *Harry Potter* was the thing my 12-year-old self needed, and the thing my 30-year-old self continues to need. *Harry Potter* is a spell to counteract the cynicism and apathy the world tries to make in us. For me, *Harry Potter* is always joy.

Harry's journey has allowed us to believe in magic—not just the magic of flying brooms, unicorns, and people being turned into ferrets or teapots into tortoises, but also the magic that we can find in new discoveries, in friendships, in good people working together to make the world better, and in ourselves. The books continue to resonate because they give readers a hope for magic in the world and within themselves, hope that we can always do better, and hope that good will ultimately win out.

LUMOS: ON DISCOVERY, WONDER, AND CYNICISM

As a child, I was sure that magic was everywhere. I was just waiting for it to find me. My sister and I spent many bruised hours jumping off the couch with blankets in our hands. Each time, we slammed down to the carpet, knees first, but we were never deterred. One of these times, if we were patient, our carpets were bound to catch magic like a match catches fire, and we'd never hit the ground.

I watched and rewatched *Matilda*, the story of the child with *powers* who could move objects with her mind. In my bedroom, I twirled and imagined the playing cards that she made rotate around her in a joyful tornado. I spent hours staring at pencils and glasses of water, hoping for a tremble. When my father wanted us to put our toys away, he'd set our dolls up overnight as if they'd been having a tea party, or rearrange our bears as if they'd been playing catch. I knew it was my father, but every so often, when he'd leave early in the morning for work,

I convinced myself that the toys had done it themselves. Magic existed, but it was tentative, private, fragile. The toys lived, and they only stopped moving when we looked. They stopped moving *because* we looked.

And then came Harry, the boy with magic beyond what I'd ever imagined. Though Harry's powers are great, and though he ends up needing those powers to face some of the most terrible dark forces in the world and within himself, some of the series' most enduring power is in the magic at its simplest.

Harry Potter and the Sorcerer's Stone is where I turn when I want to remember how it feels to be 12 and to still believe in magic. Despite everything that happens after, *Sorcerer's Stone* is my favorite book of the series because we get to tag along and experience Harry's wonder at the newness of this magical world, where he finally belongs. We find joy each time Harry discovers Diagon Alley through the Leaky Cauldron, which Muggles can't quite see; we experience his curiosity at self-stirring cauldrons, overpriced dragon liver, flying broomsticks, and goblins weighing huge rubies at Gringotts. Harry, who's gotten used to the way his life has always been, now finds newness all around him, seeing the world through a fresh-scrubbed pane of glass. And even after Harry is fully immersed in the wizarding world and some of that newness wears off, the books continue to deliver the childlike wonder, even if it comes in smaller bites—Hogsmeade, the beautiful prefects' bathroom and its taps full of magical foam and bubbles, dragons, the fantasies of being able to fly and breathe underwater, and the curiosities in the Department of Mysteries. Though Harry gets older, it's comforting to know that there are still plenty of secrets to discover.

Not everyone in the series views magical secrets as a source of possibility and discovery. During *Goblet of Fire*, Igor Karkaroff, the former Death Eater and headmaster at rival magical school Durmstrang, is worried about Viktor Krum giving away the school's secrets to Hermione. Krum and Hermione are enjoying the Yule Ball, drinking punch, and learning about each other's lives, but Karkaroff refuses to see their friendship as something innocent. He replaces his sense of learning and curiosity with jealousy, distrust, and self-involvement. Karkaroff is a version of our older selves, when we grow out of asking, "What's that?" and instead ask, "What do you want from me?"

To defend his reasoning, Igor says to Dumbledore, "Do we not jealously guard the halls of learning that have been entrusted to us? Are we not right to be proud that we alone know our school's secrets, and right to protect them?" and Dumbledore responds, "Oh I would never dream of assuming I know all Hogwarts' secrets, Igor," (*Goblet of Fire*, 417) before referencing the beautiful Room of Requirement, which, for Dumbledore, fills itself with chamber pots. Even Dumbledore, who's seen much tragedy and the best and worst of the wizarding world, is able to admit that he doesn't know everything about the Hogwarts castle, and can find new things to discover at 113 years old. We can learn from Dumbledore that a sense of childhood wonder, so easy to lose and grow out of, can be found again with curiosity; that Hogwarts continues to provide and surprise, for those who are curious and open enough to see it.

Curiosity requires the recognition that there's something you don't know, something you can still learn. Curiosity requires humility. And of the many tragedies of Voldemort's life, one of the biggest is his inability to recognize his own capacity for curiosity. Voldemort assumes that, of everyone around him, he knows the most. He's sure he knows better, and that there's no more he could possibly discover. His sense of knowledge is finite. He assumes no one else has discovered the secret of his Horcruxes or the places where he's hidden them, including Hogwarts. This assumption is part of his downfall—Harry, Dumbledore, and even Draco Malfoy have figured out the Room of Requirement. Voldemort's lack of curiosity leads to the destruction of his spirit.

That sense of curiosity and wonder extends beyond objects and magic—it's necessary to feel curiosity for the people around us, too. In *Goblet of Fire*, when the Yule Ball anxiety begins, the boys discover something new about Hermione: "But Ron was staring at Hermione as though suddenly seeing her in a whole new light. 'Hermione, Neville's right—you *are* a girl....'" (400). And this, ultimately, leads to one of Ron and Hermione's biggest fights—her fury at his not recognizing her for who she is (as more than a homework nag), and his own jealousy over Viktor Krum, along with his confusion at his own feelings. Though it leads to a fight, their new curiosity about each other as something more than just friends leads to a broader life, and to thinking about more than just themselves.

When we fail to be curious, these certain doors remain closed to us. However painful the results of exploring curiosity might seem, it's necessary for us to become more fully who we are. Harry regrets his own lack of curiosity when he learns in *Goblet of Fire* that Neville's parents had been permanently hospitalized after being tortured by Voldemort. Why, he wonders, had it never occurred to him to ask Neville about his parents, when it seems he's being raised by his grandmother? It's not that he's too shy to ask, or that he fears he might hurt Neville by asking; he has simply never thought to ask Neville about his life. Had he asked, he might have found a deeper friendship with Neville at an earlier date—the two are both orphaned in a sense, and often outcasts. And ultimately, when Neville kills Voldemort's snake Nagini, it's his help that allows Harry to win the war.

Harry trusts Neville as an important ally only when he thinks he's about to die. Had Harry been curious about Neville's life sooner, he might've gained him as a close ally much sooner, rather than at the final, most serious of moments. The trio could've become four. From Harry and Neville, we can learn to have curiosity about the most ordinary people around us, and that we might find unexpected magic in them, too.

Even after the story gets quite serious, and Harry moves from discovery to survival mode, an unexpected source still presents an innocent sense of wonder for the ordinary: Arthur Weasley. His love of Muggle objects and technology is like that of a child's. Throughout the books, we can find moments of totally unembarrassed fascination, like when he insists Vernon Dursley tell him about the "eclectic" fireplace, when he's fascinated by the subway turnstile swallowing his ticket, when he admits to collecting plugs (which he loves so much that he has hung a diagram about how to wire a plug in his office, where he can look at it every day), and when, at the Quidditch World Cup, he gets "thoroughly overexcited" when trying to use, of all things, a mallet (*Goblet of Fire,* 79).

When I first read the series as a 12-year-old nerd, I thought of Mr. Weasley's interests as too profoundly nerdy to even laugh at. He was the kind of parent I would've died of embarrassment to be around. But 18 years later, I see Mr. Weasley as often being a bright spot when things grow darkest. His love for the ordinary is a reminder to try to preserve some of that childhood sense of wonder. As we get older and more cynical, it's easy to distract ourselves from finding wonder and joy with work or with worry or with boring adult things, like piles of dishes or a dreaded call with our health insurance company or a trip to the dentist to get yet another root canal. It becomes easy to take many simple things in our lives for granted. Mr. Weasley would be overjoyed by the opportunity to use the telephone or the dentist's water gun.

Lumos is a spell that creates light where there is none to illuminate what's ahead. Curiosity is like *Lumos*—it allows us to see new things, and to see what's in front of us in a fresher, better light. Because they're discovering so many things for the first time, children look at the world with brand-new eyes, as if with a lighted wand. For them, everything new is magic. My friend's daughter loves to tell me that things are beautiful— that tiny ant crawling over her knuckle, my chipped red nail polish, my socks, a weedy white flower. Once we get used to the world, we lose that ability to enjoy newness. From each book, and especially from Mr. Weasley, we can learn the importance of creating our own magic. Part of magic is believing in the unknown, believing that the world will continue to surprise us, and resisting cynicism. Like Mr. Weasley, we can hope to find the magic in the mundane. Like my father getting up in the early-morning darkness before work to set up our teddy bears in a tea party, we have to create our own magic.

AGUAMENTI: ON HOME, FOOD, FAMILY, AND BELONGING

ϟϟϟ

I've lived in California for six years, and I still have trouble calling it home. With short stints in Spain and Boston, I spent most of my life in the snowy, gray winters and humid summers of Michigan. I also spent most of my life saying I would *never* live in California—it was simply too far. On the night before I moved, at 23 years old, I sat up late and alone on the couch at my mother's house in a yellow pool of lamplight with an atlas open on my lap. I traced the route from Michigan to California and, for the first time, really faced just how *far* away from home I would be—it was over the fold and farther than my fingers, stretched from right to left, could measure. I began to cry, but I told no one.

Harry doesn't have a home until he's 11 years old. The Dursleys let him live in a house, yes, but that physical structure and his "room" in the cupboard under the stairs are all he has.

Living with the Dursleys, Harry is neglected and abused. He is a disease to them—unwanted, ugly, and inevitable. Though we learn that the act of living with the Dursleys is part of what's keeping Harry safe and alive, keeping him alive is all they are doing. Even prisons keep people (mostly) alive.

Then Hagrid arrives with his beautiful, squashed eleventh-birthday cake for Harry, a promise of sweetness to come, and everything changes. This marks the starkest difference between the Dursleys and Harry's first real home, Hogwarts: the food. At the Dursleys, Harry is only allowed to eat whatever's left over after his cousin Dudley has had his fill, or whatever Dudley doesn't want. When Harry's punished for Dobby the house-elf's behavior (smashing Aunt Petunia's pudding) in *Chamber of Secrets*, he's locked in his room with only cold, canned soup pushed through a cat flap.

In the Dursleys' home, even the most basic thing your body needs is a symbol that Harry is worth less than the rest of the family. The Dursleys barely allow Harry to exist. And even under those circumstances, Harry is selfless: He gives the only thing he has—his leftover soggy vegetables—to his owl, Hedwig. Even though he's been denied it for almost his entire life, Harry understands that providing food is a form of love. It's all he can do, and so he does it.

When he arrives at Hogwarts, Harry is knocked out with the sheer volume and magnificence of the food at the Hogwarts feast. After the nerves of the Sorting, the feast provides comfort. In fact, year after year, Hogwarts (via the house-elves in the kitchen) brings peace through food. Maybe it seems too obvious, that food can provide comfort, but to Harry this is novel. Food is a symbol of being taken care of, of someone looking out for you, of belonging. At Hogwarts, no one gets less food or worse food than anyone else. The students are all equal, no matter what's happened to them or who their parents are; they are worthy of the same food, the same care. The feasts are a rallying, unifying place, no matter what else is happening: They bring the houses together, even if they sit separately, even after Voldemort returns.

Hogwarts is a reminder that food can be a simple way to comfort ourselves. In *Chamber of Secrets,* hot chocolate brings relief to Ginny after her ordeal, and after everything that happens to Harry over the course of that year, Dumbledore insists that "...what you need, Harry, is some food and sleep" (334). Lupin's chocolate in *Prisoner of Azkaban* helps Harry recover from Dementor attacks. And even as the Weasleys are waiting to hear whether Arthur will die from his injuries from the snake attack in *Order of the Phoenix*, the first thing that Sirius says when they finally hear he's okay is "Breakfast!" (479).

⚡⚡⚡

While the Dursleys withhold their food like they withhold their love for Harry, Molly Weasley hands out both in abundance. For Molly Weasley, home and food are one and the same. Molly's meals serve as a contrast to what Harry had been lacking—fullness, someone planning ahead and caring for him. After the summer of Dudley's diet in *Goblet of Fire*, when Harry receives even less food than usual, he finally arrives at the Burrow, sits down to Molly's familiar cooking, and thinks, "To somebody who had been living on meals of increasingly stale cake all summer, this was paradise" (61). Not *good*, not *delicious*, but *paradise*. Paradise is heaven; paradise is where you want to go after your soul leaves your body. For Harry, paradise is the Burrow.

It would be easy to write off Molly as a stereotype—a stay-at-home mom who worries that you're too skinny and makes sure you've packed clean socks. To do so, though, is a mistake. Molly is one of the unsung heroes without whom nothing would have been successful. When Harry and the Weasleys have to get up early for the Quidditch World Cup, Molly is awake and ready with breakfast. Molly feeds the Order of the Phoenix without question, at any hour of the night. She makes sure to throw Harry a birthday party anytime she can. Even after Voldemort returns and everyone is afraid for their lives, Molly opens her home and her kitchen to host Bill and Fleur's wedding, and makes sure everything is beautiful and everyone eats enough.

Molly's cooking and the Burrow enable the other characters to go out into the world and fight. She folds their laundry and she carries around her clock to keep an eye on them when every single hand is pointed at "mortal peril" (*Half-Blood Prince*, 107). Like her husband, she is a bright, necessary sun in a bleak world. To Harry, Molly and the Burrow represent far more than food—they are home; they are family; they are what allow him to live.

Though underappreciated, Molly's work extends beyond the reach of the Burrow. Harry, whether he realizes it or not, adopts her sense of generosity as a part of his own and brings it back with him to Hogwarts. When Sirius, Harry's godfather and the closest connection to Harry's parents, is running from the Ministry and hiding out in a cave in *Goblet of Fire*, Harry makes sure to send him food because he "had not forgotten what it felt like to be continually hungry" (548). When Sirius must need it the most—he's on the run, still presumed a guilty man by most of the world, alone, and living off rats—Harry extends the feeling of home and family to his godfather by sending food.

In other ways, Harry demonstrates a Molly-like generosity in the way he consistently gives up his own things for others, like when he gives his Triwizard earnings to Fred and George. He gives one of the sweaters Molly knits him to Dobby the house-elf after Dobby wishes for one, when most of the other students aren't even aware the house-elves exist. Harry's wealth could have made him suspicious and jaded, or it could have made him selfish, like it did the Dursleys. But instead, Harry chooses to use what he has to make the lives of those in his circle a little better.

Like so many women, Molly does her work quietly and thanklessly. Her lot is inherently unfair, and no one else seems to consider how they will feed themselves; they assume that Molly will take care of it. It's not until Fred and George move out that they appreciate her—and even then, it's only "now we're washing our own socks" (*Half-Blood Prince,* 339). But while Molly certainly deserves thanks, she doesn't need it to do what needs to be done. It's easy for us to feel trapped by who appreciates us or who doesn't, by who recognizes us for what we're doing. It's important to feel recognition and appreciation, and I wish people like Molly felt them more often. But in Molly's selflessness, there's power. From her, we can learn to do the work of caring for others (as parents, as teachers, as community workers, as nurses), because that work always needs to be done. We can turn away from the need to have approval for what we do. Molly Weasley can teach us that even if your work feels small or unrewarded, the good things you do ripple outward. You create a wave that rolls onward to some shore you can't ever see, but can feel its power nonetheless.

It's not until Harry, Ron, and Hermione have left home for good to fight Voldemort, camping in the Forest of Dean, that they realize what Molly gave to them. Like most things, we're unable to see how important they are until we've lost them. The fight over food, who will find it, and how they will stay alive is one of the biggest that the trio has. Food is what builds relationships, and the lack of that care is also what tears them apart.

The sharing of food is about more than just eating a meal— it's an extension of family, a community, and a cure for loneliness. When we're without that community, everything feels emptier. Food loses its taste. Back in *Goblet of Fire*, when Ron feels like Harry put his name in the Goblet for the attention and stops speaking to Harry, Harry often eats alone. There's zero description of delicious food, as if the incredible Hogwarts feasts don't register in Harry's mind at all. Once Ron comes around and he and Harry are friends again, Harry "had almost forgotten what it was like to be properly hungry" (365). Friendship and fullness are parallel. And after Sirius dies, Harry hears students in the Great Hall for dinner and, in his grief, "it seemed impossible that there could be people in the world who still desired food..." (*Order of the Phoenix*,

844). Loneliness, like hunger, affects deep us in our bodies. We need a community as badly as we need food and water.

Home can be found in a physical space—like Harry's four-poster bed in the Gryffindor boys' dormitory and Ron's room papered with Chudley Cannons posters—and in food, but home can also be found in people. What ultimately creates a sense of belonging within a family structure are the people who build that structure. At the end of *Goblet of Fire*, Harry is in the hospital wing, wracked by guilt that his insistence that Cedric Diggory take the Triwizard Cup with him is what led to Cedric's death. Mrs. Weasley says the thing that he most needs to hear: that it wasn't his fault. But it's not until Molly hugs him that Harry breaks wide open, as he rarely breaks down elsewhere, "screwing his face up against the howl of misery fighting to get out of him," because "he had no memory of ever being hugged like this, as though by a mother" (714). This love, always lacking in Harry's life, is part of the home he's trying to find. Even as we get older and tougher, and even when we pretend or think we don't need it, the need for a love like a mother's runs deep as groundwater.

But while the Weasleys are wonderful to Harry and Molly Weasley thinks of him as a son, they will never be the same as Harry's own family, as much as both might want them to be. They are the family he never had, and at the same time, they'll never be quite enough. Like Harry, even Voldemort (when he's still Tom Riddle) becomes obsessed with figuring out who his parents are, and what kind of home he might've had if he hadn't ended up an orphan. In *Goblet of Fire*, Voldemort even uses the Riddle house as a temporary headquarters. He tries to take power from the home he could've had, if his father hadn't abandoned him and his mother. But because he doesn't have a community or a family, only people who fear him or want a piece of his power, he's ultimately alone. Because of his loneliness, power is his only comfort.

And Harry, too, is ultimately alone. When Harry enters Voldemort's mind in *Order of the Phoenix* and witnesses Arthur Weasley being attacked by Nagini while on a mission for the Order, Molly Weasley is over the moon with gratitude. Without Harry, Arthur would likely have died. However, when Harry sits at the Burrow with the other Weasleys, waiting to hear whether Arthur will survive the attack or not, he feels he is an "[intruder] upon the family grief" (479). Despite how much he's part of the Weasley family, there are some ways in which he'll always be an outsider.

And that's why Harry is so joyful when he finds out that Sirius is his godfather. Finally, he will have a family of his own. When Harry finds out he could live with Sirius, "some sort of explosion took place in Harry's stomach" (*Prisoner of Azkaban*, 379). And after Harry tells Sirius he wants to go, Sirius, who's never had a family who loved him either, smiles "...the first true smile Harry had seen upon [his face]... as though a person 10 years younger were shining through the starved mask."

After Sirius dies in the battle at the Department of Mysteries in *Order of the Phoenix*, Voldemort attempts to possess Harry, hoping to get Dumbledore to mistakenly kill Harry. In Harry's grief over Sirius's death, he realizes that his own death would mean he'd get to see Sirius again. This thought, "I'll see Sirius again," is what forces Voldemort from Harry's mind.

That feeling of love and belonging and family is too much for Voldemort to take. True acceptance into a family structure is physical—we feel it in our bones.

The loss of the potential home in Sirius echoes forward into the potential loss of Hogwarts. When Hogwarts is partly destroyed in the Battle of Hogwarts, the loss is felt as deeply as the loss of a person would feel. Right before Harry walks into the woods to sacrifice himself, he sees Ginny and starts to doubt everything. "He wanted to be stopped, to be dragged back, to be sent back home.... But he was home. Hogwarts was the first and best home he had known. He and Voldemort and Snape, the abandoned boys, had all found home here" (*Deathly Hallows*, 697).

When Cedric dies, Harry sees his eyes as "blank and expressionless as the windows of a deserted house" (*Goblet of Fire*, 638)—for Harry, Cedric becomes an empty house. This is because for Harry, the soul and the home are one and the same. Living most of his life without a home was a half-life, a non-life, a kind of spiritual death. Harry sees Cedric's eyes as an empty house because, especially for Harry, the comforts of home are more than just comforts—they are necessities.

⚡⚡⚡

When my friend's father passed away suddenly, I went over to her apartment with some chocolate and a small potted plant. I didn't want to bring flowers, I thought. Flowers die. What was I doing there? I couldn't even tell. One of our other friends had ordered us dinner, so I helped unwrap it. We laid out the trays of curry and rice on her daughters' little folding table in the living room, and we sat on the floor around it in a small circle. And while food is a symbol of home and belonging and comfort and care, the food is sometimes not the point. Just like when Neville's mother hands him empty candy wrappers in the hospital, it doesn't matter that the candy itself was gone. Neville understands what his mother's gesture means and keeps the wrappers anyway (*Order of the Phoenix,* 515). The plant I brought for my friend died not too long after, but the moment of us sitting together in a circle, eating a meal together during a horrible time, is what lingers.

We can learn from this that home, like food, is temporary. Harry cannot stay at the Burrow or at Hogwarts forever. Even as late as *Deathly Hallows,* Harry yearns to find a true home. When he and Hermione have the chance to go back to Godric's Hollow, where he lived as a baby, though doesn't remember it, Harry feels a connection even deeper than the one he felt at Hogwarts: "He was about to go home, about to return to the place where he had had a family.... The life he had lost had hardly ever seemed real to him at this moment, when he knew he was about to see the place where it had been taken from him" (321). But even Godric's Hollow lets him down. His home is a monument and a ruin, not a sense of comfort.

No matter how much we fight it, our sense of home will change with time. Our childhood homes get sold. Our parents stop being able to cook for us. Family members die. The privilege of a loving home, whatever form that takes, is that we're able to take it for granted. Over and over, we must experience loss in order to learn this lesson.

It turns out that we need to create homes for ourselves. We need to make our own sense of belonging. This is why the end of the series is so moving—though I know this is opposite to what many others feel. At last, Harry finally has the home he's never quite been able to hold onto. He takes pieces of his former homes (a scar from his mother, magic from Hogwarts, his relationships with Ron and Hermione, and names from his father and Sirius), and makes the home himself.

Because I moved around so much in my twenties, I never decorated my apartment. I knew I'd just be leaving it again, and not making it truly mine made it easier to leave. But after six years in California, my husband and I have finally managed to hang up pictures and nail our bookshelves to the wall. We're saying, "This is ours, and we made it." We know the best places in town to get food when we need to feel better. Our friends feel like home.

Aguamenti is the spell that creates water, and Harry uses it in *Half-Blood Prince* to try and help Dumbledore, and later to put out Hagrid's house fire. Though we Muggles don't have *Aguamenti* to fill our cups, we can fill them instead with the things and the people we need to make a home. Like Molly Weasley, like Harry, and like Dumbledore, may we learn to create the things we need to make our own best homes. At the end of our long days, we can find comfort in the familiar space, in food, and each other. Like Dumbledore says at the end of *Prisoner of Azkaban*, we can sometimes do with a cup of tea. Or a large brandy.

PRIORI INCANTATEM: ON CONNECTING GENERATIONS

⚡⚡⚡

Every time I fly home to Michigan to celebrate Christmas with my family, I think, "This will be the year that I'll have grown up." I'll be able to drive past those same intersections I could navigate with my eyes closed without feeling that old twinge of nostalgia, recalling when the boys raced their cars and I pretended it didn't scare and thrill me. Like *Priori Incantatem*, every moment on those streets appears in front of me like a ghost. But maybe this will be the year I stop feeling 16 and start feeling 30. Maybe this year the streets will become just regular, familiar intersections, even when the same potholes smash open every year and I automatically steer around them. This year, I will be able to look at the main thoroughfare and simply notice, like anyone would, the new strip mall and the way they've made the Speedway gas station fancier with red brick, rather than picturing the way everything used to be. I'll move on, and moving on will be the okay and right thing to do.

The characters in Harry Potter feel like my bricked-over hometown. They are the past as much as they are the present. They are three things at once—their current selves, trying to survive and find happiness; the ghosts of their own parents, whether they were loved well or not; and every one of their past selves, each living beneath the last, a facade painted over and over but never quite gone. They, too, want to wave hello to their pasts and then walk away without that twinge, eyes forward.

For children, adults in their world work as the gateways to understanding the past and the world around them. Adults, though, however well-meaning, and often while trying to protect children, would rather keep this gateway closed. In the first few books, we see a deep divide between children and adults. Adults keep the truth from children, and thus the children misunderstand what's happening around them. Harry, Hermione, and Ron are constantly making mistakes while they try to figure out what's going on in their world (though Hermione is right far more often than she gets credit for). Particularly with Snape, Harry often looks for the worst possible explanation. For example, in *Prisoner of Azkaban*, he thinks Snape's glances at Professor Lupin over dinner mean that Snape wants Lupin's job, when really Snape is making sure his Wolfsbane potion worked, and that Lupin is feeling okay. And in *Sorcerer's Stone*, the trio thinks that Snape is trying to steal the Stone instead of trying to stop the theft. It's not the trio's fault, of course—like all children, they are doing their best with the little information they've been given. Writing this, I bristle at the word "children" like Harry bristles when, in *Goblet of Fire*, Fleur Delacour refers to him as a little boy. Even when we *are* young, especially once we become teenagers, we don't feel young. Our emotions run so deep that we trust them completely to teach us about the world.

While teenagers are, of course, ridiculous (how many times do we roll our eyes at Harry's uncontrollable angst in *Order of the Phoenix*?), the adults make the divide worse by not trusting children and not taking them seriously. How does it feel when you're 15 and so in love with someone that you can barely even stand to look at them, and an adult laughs at you and tells you it's just puppy love? We dismiss children's feelings because they're no longer our own, but that dismissal makes children retreat from us further. As Dumbledore says in *Order of the Phoenix*, "Youth cannot know how age thinks and feels. But old men are guilty if they forget what it was to be young" (826). Over and over again in the series, we see adults not believing young people, at their own peril. At the end of *Prisoner of Azkaban*, Minister of Magic Cornelius Fudge refuses to believe Harry's insistence on Sirius's innocence: "'Harry, Harry, you're very confused, you've been through a dreadful ordeal, lie back down, now, we've got everything under control...'YOU HAVEN'T!' Harry yelled. 'YOU'VE GOT THE WRONG MAN'" (389). Harry's fury is that of all of us at 13, when we know we have something important to say and the adults refuse to listen to us. As Dumbledore says, "There is not a shred of proof to support Black's story, except your word—and the word of two 13-year-old wizards will not convince anybody" (392).

This lack of trust is a mistake. Often, the impulse to hide the truth from young people is protective, like when Molly Weasley doesn't want her children or Harry hearing the details of the Order of the Phoenix. Her silence is her shield for them.

But each time the adults refuse to take the teenagers seriously, their own understanding of the situation is limited. They are crippling both the children and themselves. The teenagers find out the information anyway (often through eavesdropping, as with Fred and George's ingenious Extendable Ears). They want to know, but their knowledge is incomplete and fragmented, which can lead them into even more danger—like through the trapdoor underneath Fluffy, the three-headed dog.

When the adults don't believe the children, their knowledge, too, is incomplete and fragmented. Had Fudge believed Harry about Sirius Black's innocence, Peter Pettigrew might not have escaped and might not have been able to help Voldemort return to power. Hardly anyone believes Harry about Voldemort's return in *Order of the Phoenix*. In *Half-Blood Prince*, Professor McGonagall doesn't believe Harry's theories about Malfoy being a Death Eater and trying to harm someone in the castle. In all cases, had the adults listened and acted sooner, they might have headed off whatever violence was coming much more quickly. For example, when, in *Order of the Phoenix*, Harry sees a vision of Arthur Weasley being attacked by Nagini, McGonagall believes him and goes for help immediately. If someone had told Harry he was having a nightmare and should go to bed, Arthur would have died. Believing Harry is what saves Arthur's life. Dumbledore is one of the few who consistently believes Harry, and without this belief, none of the events of the story would have been set in motion.

We are throwing away a chance at deeper understanding when we don't give young people agency. Even Voldemort, an extremely intelligent teenager himself, made this mistake. In

Half-Blood Prince, when Harry and Dumbledore are retrieving the locket Horcrux from the underground lake, Dumbledore realizes that Voldemort never thought an underage wizard could've broken through his defenses, and so he didn't prepare for Harry. Dumbledore says, "Age is foolish when it underestimates youth" (564–65). Voldemort's oversight became his own weakness.

It's incredible that, as adults, we continue to underestimate young people when our own childhoods are not as far away as they might seem. As the series progresses, the generations start to collide and collapse. Harry's presence, and later Voldemort's, forces the adults to double back and consider their past selves. The adults seemingly become less adult.

Up until *Prisoner of Azkaban*, Snape has been flitting around the castle, and except for saving Harry's life from Defense Against the Dark Arts Professor Quirinus Quirrell in the first year, he is easy to understand. He is a cruel and annoying grownup to Harry, Ron, and Hermione, and prefers his fellow Slytherins. He is like the math teacher I hated in seventh grade, who mocked me for not understanding fractions. Even now, some 20 years later, when I see a fraction it begins to fade, and it's her face and her cloud of blonde hair that I see instead. She was an adult; she was the teacher; she was supposed to know better; and so I hated her. Characters like Snape and my math teacher make the perfect enemies because they are not complicated.

But Snape's memory is long. When Snape discovers that Sirius Black has returned, Snape is not the adult anymore. He is not the man who trusts Dumbledore's judgment above all else.

When he sees Sirius, the adult Snape fades into his 16-year-old self, who sees the handsome bully returning to torment him some more. When Dumbledore believes Harry's story that Sirius is innocent of the murder of Peter Pettigrew, Snape says, "You surely don't believe a word of Black's story?... Sirius Black showed he was capable of murder at the age of 16" (*Prisoner of Azkaban,* 391). In *Order of the Phoenix*, Snape and Sirius trade insults in the kitchen at Grimmauld Place, and they end up drawing wands on each other when Sirius calls Snape his cruel childhood nickname—Snivellus. Sirius finds that old cruelty within himself, locates that old bruise within Snape, and presses. But at the same time, Snape's young self, the self that is in love with Lily Potter, still lives within him, and this is part of what keeps Harry safe year after year, even as Snape can't help tormenting him. Every time Snape looks at Harry, he must see all his former selves spooled out in front of him—his lonely childhood, his one friend in Lily Potter, Lily Potter turning her back on him, his own turn toward and then away from the Death Eaters, and then grief that seeing Harry's face simultaneously heals and creates. When Sirius returns, Snape cannot grow up. He is 16 again. He is trying to make sense of the fraction in front of him and cannot.

On the other hand, while Snape reminds us that we can't escape our childhood hurts, Lupin reminds us that that might be okay. Lupin's childhood self is what saves Sirius Black's life. Even before Lupin knows the truth about Sirius's innocence, and while the teachers feel enough danger to allow Dementors to patrol the school, he refuses to tell Dumbledore that Sirius is an Animagus and could use this ability to get into Hogwarts. He refuses because doing so would mean that he'd have to let Dumbledore know that Lupin, in his desire for friendship as a child, had left the Shrieking Shack repeatedly, and had thus broken Dumbledore's rules. As Lupin says, "Dumbledore's trust while I was at school has meant everything to me" (*Prisoner of Azkaban,* 356). Even knowing Lupin was a werewolf, Dumbledore let him come to Hogwarts as a child (with precautions for the other students), and gave him respect and a job as an adult.

Lupin's childhood self, who was shunned and discriminated against but finally found acceptance at Hogwarts because of Dumbledore, reached forward into adulthood and kept Lupin silent. This, though, is what saved Sirius—had Lupin fought his childhood instincts and gone to Dumbledore sooner, before either of them knew that he was innocent, Sirius might have been sent to Azkaban, or worse, to the Dementors. Lupin's childhood self knew better.

Some might read Lupin's hesitance as cowardice, especially because Lupin is sometimes a bystander when he has a chance to act. "Why not protect the students against Sirius," they might ask, "who everyone assumed was a mass murderer chasing after Harry?" It's a fair point. Lupin should have, perhaps, known better. But in that moment, his childhood self reciprocated the friendship he received as a boy. Whether intentional or not, it saved Sirius's life, and gave Harry a glimpse of a family.

It's tempting to blame Snape and Lupin for their behaviors, to say that they're trapped in the past and that they (and that we) need to let things go and to grow up. But that's easier said than done, and I'm not sure it's right, either. It doesn't matter whether we should or can let go. Even 17 years after the Battle of Hogwarts, when they meet with their children on platform 9¾, Harry and Malfoy still can't stop themselves from hating each other. We see in them that we can never escape our childhood selves. They are our companions, whether they keep us company or warn us away from pain.

In the same way that we can never quite grow out of our childhood selves, we can never grow out of our parents, either. Harry, without having a clear memory of his parents, is fixated upon preserving their memory and the things for which they died. At first, he has a pure idea of who his parents are: heroes in the resistance against Voldemort, a Quidditch hero and a Charms darling, unquestionably good. He's constantly told by his professors, Dumbledore, and Hagrid how great his mother and father were. When Harry is in his moments of deepest peril (like when his wand against Voldemort's creates *Priori Incantatem*, and when Harry walks to his death in the Forbidden Forest), he looks to his parents for guidance.

Harry spends much of his first few years at Hogwarts trying desperately to live up to his parents' legacy, and feeling like he can never possibly be as good and as brave as they were. Neville, too, has the same struggle against the legacy of his parents. In addition to Neville's fear of Snape, his fear that he's not brave enough for Gryffindor, and his memory blunders, in *Order of the Phoenix*, Neville mentions to Harry that "Gran's always telling Professor Marchbanks I'm not as good as my dad" (707). Like all teenagers, they fight against the feeling that they are utterly average. When they compare themselves to their parents, they always let themselves down. Neville and

Harry are forever trying to be their parents, and yet feel they will never quite reach them.

Later, though, Harry must grapple with the fact that his parents were human—his father sometimes *was* arrogant, and his mother didn't love James at first. He's forced to question that his parents, only 21 years old when they died, might not be the heroes he wants to live up to. If he's not looking to them as a guide, where should he look? Sirius and Lupin, haunted by their own childhood selves, complicate Harry's relationship to his parents and try to insist that he turn into the kind of man that *they* think his parents wanted him to be. In *Order of the Phoenix*, when Sirius wants to meet up with Harry and Harry is too worried for Sirius's safety to say yes, Sirius says, "The risk would've been what made it fun for James" (305). In *Deathly Hallows*, when Lupin wants to come with the trio on their Horcrux quest (and leave his pregnant wife, Tonks, behind), he says, "Harry, I'm sure James would have wanted me to stick with you" (212).

By this time, though, Harry's tired of hearing people tell him how to understand his own family legacy. Though Lupin might have been saying that Harry's father would have wanted Lupin to watch out for Harry, Harry sees it again as a kind of reckless foolhardiness. Perhaps because he recognizes this sometimes destructive tendency of his father's in himself, Harry feels manipulated. "'Well,' said Harry slowly, 'I'm not. I'm pretty sure my father would have wanted to know why you aren't sticking with your own kid, actually'" (212). In this moment, Harry is done being told how he should be. He's tired of constantly being measured against the history of his parents.

When Harry tells Sirius to stay home, it's not because he's a wet blanket or a wimp. It's because Harry is an orphan, desperate to keep his father figure alive. He's not like James, someone who doesn't have a sense of what risk means. For Harry, fun is not part of the equation. Harry knows exactly the loss that he risks by putting Sirius in danger. When Harry rebuffs Lupin for wanting to go adventuring, he's decided who his parents are and finally feels like he understands them, but also recognizes himself as separate from them. He doesn't allow the legacy of his parents to speak for him anymore. Their life will always be an important part of his, but it will not be the only thing about him.

While Harry wants to figure out where he fits in his parents' legacy, others want to escape from their own heritage and the ways it shames them. Voldemort and Snape are both haunted by their half-blood parentage, as Sirius is haunted by his pure-blood family, and they all try their best to run from their heritage—though of course, it's difficult to outrun blood. Malfoy becomes a Death Eater like his father. And even Dumbledore fights his own past: After his father Percival was sent to Azkaban for attacking Muggles to defend his daughter, Dumbledore's sister Ariana, the wizarding world spread rumors about Percival's hatred of Muggles. Dumbledore pushes back against this false history by fighting for the rights of Muggles and trying to see the good in everyone.

Somehow, these acts of escape work as acts of preservation. In trying *not* to be like their families, the characters find themselves. Once Harry and Neville stop trying to live up to their parents' legacies and start making their own way, they become braver and more like their parents anyway. They become their parents as they become more themselves. As McGonagall says to Neville in *Half-Blood Prince*, "It's high time your grandmother learned to be proud of the grandson she's got, rather than the one she thinks she ought to have" (174). Whether we're trying to honor our parents or distance ourselves from their mistakes, their legacy is what drives us to become who we are. Our parents live on through us, whether we want them to or not.

Our parents shape us into the people we are as children, and the people we are as children continue to live within us. Even now that I'm 30 years old, when I go home to visit, my mother wants to make me tea the same way she did when I was young. I let her. When my father makes me breakfast, I set the table with the same grapefruit spoons I used as a child to drink the leftover sugared juice.

When we go home, perhaps that twinge of nostalgia is a necessary kind of pain. Some parts of our hearts never do grow up, and that is a gift. Our younger selves living within can help us remember what it was like to be young. They can help us remember the crushes that hurt—really, physically hurt, somewhere between our ribs and our bellies—and the times we understood things that the adults thought we didn't. The adults in our lives and the children we were can teach us the humility of believing kids. Like in *Harry Potter*, when we take kids seriously, we can avoid making the same mistakes. By listening to where we came from, we can illuminate where we must go.

FIDELIUS: ON BETRAYAL
AND LOYALTY

When I was in seventh grade, I liked a boy who was out of my league. He was so far out of my league that whenever I would see him in the hallway, I would turn and literally run away. His face was like the sun—beautiful, dangerous, best not to look directly at for too long. But he was kind to me, and even laughed at a joke I made in social studies once. And not a cruel laugh, either; he gave me the kindness of a genuine laugh. I still remember the moment, with my back twisted to face him, sitting behind me, his smile way too good for braces.

Right before the school dance, he called me and asked me to go with him.

I might have cried or maybe not, but I certainly stammered something uncool into the phone and made sure that I said yes, of course, as if this wasn't a life-shattering kind of good fortune. I didn't doubt it for a second—why shouldn't my dream come true? Why couldn't it happen to me?

But you see where this is headed, right? On the day of the dance, I came to school in my best blue eyeshadow that I thought made me look hot, and my brightest lime-green velour T-shirt. I couldn't wait to see my date in third hour. Before I could, though, my friend Melissa took pity on me. In second hour, she told me that it had all been a lie. It hadn't been that boy calling me, but had actually been another friend's little brother. She wanted to tell me before I made an idiot out of myself, going up and talking to a popular boy as if that were normal.

The worst part was not the situation with the boy, which had only ever turned out as I expected, but that all my friends had been in on it. They thought it would be fun. Their loyalty was to each other, not to me. Perhaps Melissa's gesture of telling me the truth was a moment of teenage-girl mercy, but it didn't matter. I thought then that she must've done it just to make her own ego feel better. I was too stung for mercy.

Don't feel too bad for me, though. At lunch that same day, I left the friends who'd bullied me and sat with better, kinder people. The middle-school betrayal taught me something necessary—you can sometimes put your trust in the wrong people. But even if it's betrayed, that trust is worth it. My cruel friends set me on a path toward new, better, more loyal friends, some who are still sticking with me, even some 20 years later. Their decision to root themselves near me, no matter the many things that try to tear them away, is a form of love.

Harry's sense of loyalty is one of his driving impulses. Because he's had to grow up without parents, without that sense that someone will stick with you no matter what, Harry views betrayal as a kind of unforgivable sin. For Harry, you should never leave those you care about. You stay with them and support them, whether it's the logical and right thing to do or not.

It's a beautiful kind of symmetry, then, that Harry's first encounter with the magical world is with the most loyal friend you could find—Hagrid. Long before Harry, Hagrid was "Dumbledore's man through and through" (*Half-Blood Prince,* 348). In *Goblet of Fire,* when the Durmstrang headmaster Igor Karkaroff is furious with Dumbledore, he says, "...here's what I think of you!" (562) and spits at his feet. Hagrid then grabs Karkaroff by the collar, lifts him off his feet, and slams him into a tree and demands an apology. Hagrid's loyalty to Dumbledore is such that he won't tolerate any kind of disrespect to Dumbledore, even from a former Death Eater, someone we might expect to be disrespectful. To Hagrid, it doesn't matter. Dumbledore always respects and supports him, so he does the same for Dumbledore. Hagrid owes the life he lives mostly to Dumbledore. He protects what's important to him, no exception.

Not only is Hagrid loyal to Dumbledore, who's supported and protected him, but he's also fiercely loyal to Harry. Hagrid doesn't owe anything to Harry—the opposite, in fact. If anything, Harry partly owes his life to Hagrid (though Hagrid *does* toy with Harry's life a little, with dragon eggs and Blast-Ended Skrewts). It was Hagrid who fought through the wreckage of the Potters' house, cried over Lily's and James's bodies, and rescued the somehow unbroken baby before Death Eaters could find him. Hagrid stands by Harry, even when the Goblet of Fire spits out his name: "'You believe I didn't do it, then?' said Harry, concealing with difficulty the rush of gratitude he felt at Hagrid's words. 'Course I do,' Hagrid grunted. 'Yeh say it wasn' you, an' I believe yeh'" (*Goblet of Fire*, 294–95). Hagrid believes Harry that Voldemort's come back. Even when Hagrid thinks Harry has died, he stays with him, carrying Harry in his arms the same way he did when Harry was an infant; Hagrid's loyalty is unselfish. It does not need an audience.

In return, Harry becomes loyal to Hagrid, too; Hagrid's loyalty to Harry is returned to him threefold. Harry extends his care for Hagrid by introducing Ron and Hermione to Hagrid, drawing them together as if under the Invisibility Cloak. Thanks to Harry, the rest of the trio quickly becomes as loyal to Hagrid as he is. After Hagrid becomes the Care of Magical Creatures professor, the trio stays loyal to him and supports him even as things unravel, and even when it becomes clear that he's not always the greatest professor. Hermione remains loyal to Hagrid as he's falsely accused of negligence when Buckbeak the hippogriff attacks Malfoy. Harry and Ron are, at the time, distracted by the mysterious arrival of the Firebolt, and forget about their loyalty, but Hermione even cuts into her precious studying time at the library and gives some of it to Hagrid, researching law for Buckbeak's case. Hermione's loyalty is selfless. And by the time Hagrid is forced to leave under Umbridge, the trio continues to protect Hagrid by lying about his whereabouts. From the trio and Hagrid, we can learn the lesson of selfless loyalty to those we love. We can love each other by showing up, no matter what.

But loyalty is a complex and difficult path. Sometimes our loyalties must change—and, depending on which side you're on, a change in loyalty can feel like a betrayal. Perhaps one of the biggest betrayals in the book is the wizarding world's betrayal of Harry. From *Goblet of Fire* through *Half-Blood Prince*, the people who always believed in Harry as the Boy Who Lived—their symbol for the possibility of triumph over Voldemort, their symbol of innocence and goodness—lose faith in the human boy behind their symbol. As he gets older, they want him to live up to his own miracle. And he does: Over and over again, he survives. But to them, survival becomes less of a miracle the second time around. And after all, isn't that what they're doing, too—surviving? While rumors of Voldemort fly around, Harry should do something, they believe. Harry should also shut up. Harry is not good enough and Harry is too much. Can we blame him for his angst in *Order of the Phoenix*? Helped along by the *Daily Prophet* and a Ministry of Magic more selfish and fearful than brave, the wizarding world loses their loyalty toward Harry Potter. It *should* be easy to stay loyal to Harry and the goodness he stands for, but they teach us how easily our sense of loyalty can be broken—when we're afraid, it's easier to abandon our loyalties.

Instead, though, when we're afraid, we should think carefully about our loyalties. Are we most loyal to ourselves and our own motives? Are we most loyal to the way things were, rather than the way they could be? Sometimes, we can't know whether, like with Harry's parents, our loyalty is misplaced. And sometimes, loyalty requires bravery. In *Order of the Phoenix*, we see Luna Lovegood and Ernie Macmillan, a Hufflepuff in Harry's year, agree, publicly, to support Harry's story that Voldemort has returned. Almost no one agrees with them at this point, other than Ron and Hermione, Hagrid, and Dumbledore. There is hardly any proof, other than his word, to show that Harry's story is true. Luna and Ernie have nothing to go on but their sense of loyalty to what Harry represents—resistance to evil and a willingness to face the truth, no matter how awful that truth might be. Luna and Ernie's loyalty is a kind of faith, belief without proof. Like them, we can try to be loyal, even when it might cost us.

Some might say this kind of loyalty is naive. Perhaps it feels safer to protect yourself with cynicism. But Luna and Ernie's support of Harry is more than blind faith—it works like a draft of *Felix Felicis*. It gives Harry the strength to keep going and to be loyal to his own mission, knowing that someone is there with him, especially those who don't feel obligated to be there (like Ron and Hermione may).

One of the most obvious symbols of loyalty in the book is the *Fidelius Charm*: "... the magical concealment of a secret inside a single, living soul" (*Prisoner of Azkaban,* 205). It requires that one person, the Secret-Keeper, be unflinchingly loyal to another. In our world, loyalty is a form of secret-keeping—we have trust that those loyal to us will keep our secrets safe, and we do our best to do the same. For Lily and James Potter, even if their loyalty ended up hurting them, their sense of trust and belief in their friends lives on through Sirius, and then through Harry. From Luna and Ernie, we can learn that it's worth it to have that sense of trust and loyalty in someone or something, even when we can't know whether we've made the right call. A cynical, suspicious, fearful life, like those of Cornelius Fudge or Peter Pettigrew, is not much of a life at all.

Loyalty is not always simple, loving, or uncomplicated. It's not always one thing or another; loyalty versus betrayal, a good thing versus a bad one. In *Prisoner of Azkaban*, when Harry learns (incorrectly, as we later discover) that Sirius Black betrayed his parents to Voldemort, his immediate reaction is rage. He's not worried about his own safety or about Sirius's background as a criminal; he's furious because he believes Sirius manipulated his parents' loyalty. Harry's parents trusted Sirius, and it killed them. Harry sees Sirius's betrayal as a betrayal of him, too—Sirius's betrayal of their loyalty made Harry an orphan. And this sense of loyalty to his parents' lives and to the life he could have had is what drives Harry.

The adults in his life are worried Harry will go after Sirius. Hermione says, "'Don't be silly...Harry doesn't want to kill anyone, do you, Harry?' Again, Harry didn't answer. He didn't know what he wanted to do. All he knew was that the idea of doing nothing, while Black was at liberty, was almost more than he could stand" (*Prisoner of Azkaban*, 215). Harry's intense sense of loyalty nearly makes him a killer. The darker side of loyalty is the desire for revenge. No matter how many leaders hurt people in the name of loyalty, we never quite learn this lesson.

But Harry does. Before he learns the truth, Harry is finally able to corner Sirius, and Harry points his wand straight at Sirius's chest. Perhaps Harry's also driven by the pressure of his own legacy; perhaps he feels a bit responsible, since the wizarding world is loyal to him as their hero, and he doesn't want to let them down. Letting Sirius go free would feel like a betrayal of himself.

But here is where Harry stops to think about his devotion to loyalty. Though they're interrupted by Lupin's arrival, Harry gets his wand back and has a second chance to hurt Sirius. But rather than attempting to kill Sirius to avenge his parents, he lets Sirius speak and tell him the truth of what happened. When he does so, Harry defines the limits of his own loyalty—he refuses to be blindly loyal to his parents for the sake of loyalty alone. Instead, he forms a new sense of loyalty—he stays loyal to his own moral code, rather than a simple understanding of loyalty and retribution. In a different way, he stays loyal to his parents and their sense of morality when he realizes he does not want to kill Sirius over the sense of betrayal he felt. Harry's loyalty is to truth, to his parents, however flawed.

So perhaps it is no surprise that we then learn that Sirius's definition of loyalty is even stricter than Harry's. When we get the real story of Harry's parents' deaths—that it was in fact Peter Pettigrew who betrayed them and sold them out to Voldemort, not Sirius—Peter wonders whether there was any point to resisting Voldemort. He says that Voldemort would've killed him if he hadn't given him information, and Sirius screams at him, "Then you should have died...rather than betray your friends, as we would have done for you" (*Prisoner of Azkaban,* 375). For Sirius, loyalty toward friends is more important than his own safety. Rather than saving yourself in order to save others, Sirius believes you must sacrifice yourself in your loyalty for others. Do not put your own oxygen mask on before assisting others. You give away the oxygen to someone who deserves it more than you, and you go down with the plane.

I'm not sure if we should be as brave as Sirius. When should we sacrifice ourselves? Are we any good if we are gone, too? For all of us, we have people in our lives we would gladly die to protect. For Sirius, whose blood family is cruel to him, James and Lily *are* his family. They are worth dying for. And for Ron, too, who puts his body on the line for Harry when he volunteers to play the life-sized wizard chess, sacrifice is necessary. Perhaps it is the highest form of love to say that someone else's life is worth as much as yours, sometimes more.

Maybe our lesson from Sirius, Hagrid, Dumbledore, and the trio is not that we must die for those we feel loyal to, but rather, that we've got to be loyal to whatever is most important to us. We can define the boundaries of our loyalties ourselves. That loyalty is a love letter to others, but it's even more of a love letter to ourselves. Loyalty can shift—we can't always know where to place our loyalties, and sometimes we'll make mistakes. We can replace our old, flawed loyalties with ones that do more good, even ones that scare us with their newness. Our loyalties are faith in each other. Our presence for each other says *I believe you, I see you.* Loyalty is defining what is most important to you, and guarding it as best you can.

LEGILIMENS: ON GOOD PEOPLE AND DEATH EATERS

My grandmother used to steal things. Not shoplifting, exactly, but not the extra bottle of hotel toiletries, either. She used to steal the occasional beautiful spoon from a restaurant, or the bottle of special seasoning salt you could only find on the tables at Big Boy diners—things no one would miss, things it didn't hurt to lose, things that brought small joys to her everyday life. My grandmother was also a smart and kind person.

As an adult, I've picked up my grandmother's habit. I love small sugar spoons and cups, in particular. I took a beautifully carved glass from one of my friend's wedding tables. I told my friend and she shrugged, and said they wouldn't miss it. I did not feel bad as I put it in my purse; it didn't hurt the vendor, and it brought me a small bit of joy. My whole life, I have identified as a Good Girl. The cup felt like a reward the world owed me. It felt good to do something, for once, that wasn't very good at all. Like Harry, when he sneaks out of the Gryffindor common room at night, or when he ignores his lack of a permission slip and goes to Hogsmeade anyway, this kind of small crime feels like no problem. If being good is like a ladder, then Harry and I are perhaps only one step down from the top.

As a child I had a lying problem, long before the petty theft. Not serious lies, of course, but I worked in what I thought were small, unprovable lies. I'd tell my friends that a boy they didn't know told me I was pretty. Or that my great-great-grandfather was famous. When message boards were still a thing, I frequented one that someone said Rupert Grint would occasionally visit. He had been there once and posted a brief one-sentence reply to someone that seemed genuine enough, and the entire message board (myself included) hung around for months and months afterward, hoping to dip a toe into the edge of his spotlight and be made brighter from it ourselves. At some point, I told my friends that Rupert Grint had responded to something that I'd said. I can't remember the lie exactly, now, but likely it was that I was funny or cool or unique, or some other thing that I was desperate to be singled out for.

Thinking back, I'm certain the lie was as transparent as I felt—it began to fall apart almost immediately. But I wanted someone to notice me, make me visible and more myself, choose me and say *you*, and my middle-school self was willing to lie to get what she wanted. Like Harry, who frequently lies to his friends and his professors, these lies felt self-protective. Harry wanted to keep things to himself, or to do things he shouldn't, and I wanted to make myself into someone I wasn't.

We step down one more rung on the ladder, but even so, the lies felt worth that.

And perhaps worst of all, I once wanted to hurt my sister. Most siblings fight, yes, but my sister and I didn't. We were best friends. Even now, we like to tell people that we can count the big fights we've had on one hand. This was one of them: She was in my room, pushing my buttons in the way that only someone who knows you intimately can, and I felt my face get hotter and hotter, and then I boiled over. I wanted her out. I grabbed her by the shirt, lifted her, and physically threw her out of my room. She slammed into the cabinet doors on the opposite side of the hallway so hard that one was knocked off its hinges, and she fell to the ground. I couldn't get the loud *bang* her body made out of my head. I apologized and apologized right after, but it didn't matter. I think of myself then the same way I think of Harry after he uses the Half-Blood Prince's *Sectumsempra* spell on Malfoy. Though Harry wanted to hurt Malfoy (and though Malfoy had been about to use an Unforgivable Curse), he hadn't *really* meant to hurt him. He'd lost control. Harry stands over Malfoy's bleeding body and is horrified at what he was capable of. With my sister, I'd done damage, and I couldn't take that back. She wasn't hurt, but the desire to do damage is what terrified me. But in that moment, I discovered that some parts of me were not always good. Many times since, I've had to learn this lesson.

Harry Potter might seem like the ultimate good-versus-evil story, and in many ways, it is. Every time I read the series, I feel comforted knowing that good will battle evil and eventually, good will win out, and everything will be okay. This is the secret wish we all carry for our own lives, no matter our other beliefs, that someday things will untangle and all will be well and good again.

But looking at the series a bit more closely, the line between good and evil is *not* always so clear. As the characters get older, that line blurs more and more. With a few exceptions (namely Hermione and Bellatrix Lestrange), most of the other characters tread somewhere in between good and evil—Harry and Dumbledore most of all. And even Voldemort, evil as he is, still holds remnants of the child he used to be within, the good child he might have been. This could be the flayed creature that Harry sees in *Deathly Hallows*—that little bit of possible goodness that exists, tiny and unwanted, within Voldemort.

As Sirius says, "The world isn't split into good people and Death Eaters" (*Order of the Phoenix,* 302). The lesson the characters learn is the same one we have to learn again and again—that we are not always as good as we think we are, that we are as capable of great evil as great good. *Legilimens* is the spell used to read minds, and that's what the series asks the characters and the readers to do for ourselves: Look into our own minds, and examine it all, whether we like what we see or not. Although the series appears to present a fight between good and evil, dividing *us* versus *them* in as many ways as possible, instead, the series teaches us to fight the evil within ourselves.

However, rather than understanding the gray areas that exist between good and evil and between ourselves and others, it's much easier to insist that things are black and white; easier to make divisions *between* ourselves and others instead of searching for the divisions within ourselves. The Dursleys do it from the beginning—they are obsessed with who is "normal" and who is not. They form ranks with those they feel are normal like them, and literally pretend anyone who doesn't fit into their sense of normalcy doesn't exist. But we, the readers, are equally guilty of such judgments. Though all of us are occasionally guilty of some Dursleyish behavior, we love to hate them. We are glad when Harry finally escapes— he seems clearly good, and the Dursleys are clearly bad. We immediately sort ourselves into Houses alongside the Hogwarts students and make our own ranks—you're either with us, or you're not. Your house is the good guys, and everyone else isn't quite as good.

Even Hagrid—beautiful, kind, accepting Hagrid—draws a line. He often mocks Muggles in front of the trio, and he sees no room for gray areas or redemption from dark magic. The easier thing to do is to stay among people you perceive are like you, and to say more firmly, "We are better because we are this and not that." In *Prisoner of Azkaban*, before they realized Sirius was innocent, Hagrid talks about him like this: "...when a wizard goes over ter the dark side, there's nothin' and no one that matters to 'em anymore" (207).

But the series hints that this isn't always true. For example, Narcissa Malfoy, in a family often making evil choices, still makes a very good one—she indirectly helps Harry defeat Voldemort. At the end of *Deathly Hallows*, when Narcissa Malfoy feels Harry's still-beating heart, she denies the chance for evil (letting Voldemort know Harry's still alive), and instead uses the moment to get information about her son (726). She lies to Voldemort, and this allows Harry to get carried out, away from the forest, where the battle can begin again in earnest. The thing that matters to her in that moment is not Voldemort or power or pure blood—it's her son. Even though she's done terrible things, she cares about those she loves more than the evil that tempts her. That's the spark of goodness that turns their family away from following Voldemort.

And even the Dursleys might possess a spark of good. Despite their intolerance and their fears, they still take in Harry as a baby. This does not excuse the way they treat him as he grows up. But the fact remains that even cruel people can have some bit of goodness within. It's hard for me to write this, as I'd rather just think of the Dursleys as evil. But in order to confront evil, we can try to understand it by recognizing the goodness between the roots of evil, just like the evil tendencies within ourselves.

Much more important than Narcissa's or the Dursleys' bit of good, though, is Snape's. Despite all the ways in which Snape is evil—joining the Death Eaters, telling Voldemort about the prophecy that leads to Lily and James' deaths, his many cruelties to the trio (especially Harry and Hermione)—Snape uses most of his adult life, including his very last moments, to do good for Lily and for Harry. Snape's love of Lily Potter is what drives him to double-cross Voldemort, though he must know it will eventually lead to his own death. And though Harry clings to his own understanding of Snape as evil for nearly seven years, Snape's bit of goodness forms a protective embrace around Harry year after year. On his deathbed, he does a profound kindness by giving Harry the truth he needs, the truth Harry has craved from the beginning, to do what he must. Snape's goodness is giving Harry both the information he needs in order to survive, and the truth that Harry needs to fully understand himself and Lily. Harry can now see Snape and Lily for who they were—neither bad nor good, but fallible and human. When we insist on drawing lines between who is good and who is bad, we blind ourselves to seeing each other and ourselves fully.

At the same time, the books demonstrate the idea that good and evil are muddy, and thus, thinking "we're all the same" isn't quite right, either. Harry refuses to work with the Ministry in *Half-Blood Prince* and *Deathly Hallows*, since they've called him a liar and ignored the fact of Voldemort's return—a kind of evil of ignorance. He's not willing to offer unity for unity's sake alone. This shows that even if we're not in direct opposition, we don't have to get along.

Part of the complication of good and evil is that we might have to recognize our differences and leave them be. We see this in Harry and Draco Malfoy. In another kind of story, Harry and Malfoy might bond through their shared struggles and end up as best friends. Harry might be pulled toward evil, like Dumbledore was with the dark wizard Gellert Grindelwald, or he might pull Malfoy over to his side. But this is not that story. As the books go on, Malfoy strays more and more toward evil—joining the Death Eaters, being willing to kill Dumbledore, and even threatening to kill Harry in the Malfoys' cellar in *Deathly Hallows* (though his voice shakes, unsure, while he does it). But ultimately, even when Malfoy and Harry are trapped in the Room of Requirement together, about to die in the flames, Malfoy still doesn't aim to kill. And Harry, though it would be easy to let Malfoy die, thinks, "What a terrible way to die...he had never wanted this" (632).

Though they hate each other, they are willing to let some of it go, to step toward the line between them and reach out toward one another. Still, despite that, at the end of the books, Harry and Malfoy are still not friends. They are not unified. They understand that they are both more than true good or true evil, and they are bound by their history together, but they do not need to get along.

Though the fight for good seems simple, in *Goblet of Fire*, we learn that sometimes, our quest to be good has the opposite effect: We meet evil with more evil. Just as characters who seem evil might still have some humanity within, those who seem good are not fully so, either. During the first war against Voldemort, Barty Crouch, whose own son was convicted of being a Death Eater, begins to allow harsher and harsher punishments for Voldemort supporters. Eventually, the Aurors are allowed to kill Death Eaters on sight, instead of just capturing them. Sirius tells Harry that "times like that bring out the best in some people and the worst in others. Crouch's principles might have been good in the beginning... Crouch fought violence with violence... I would say he became as ruthless and cruel as many on the Dark side..." (*Goblet of Fire*, 527). As his son is dragged off to Azkaban in front of a celebrating courtroom crowd, Crouch screams that he has no son at all (596). His devotion to appearing good and to justice is so great that he's willing to call for his own son's death— and assert that he never lived at all. Sometimes good can look a lot like evil.

Even Ron can demonstrate the way good and evil live within us all, and might sometimes be hard to distinguish: In *Deathly Hallows*, he suggests (if half-heartedly) that they kill two

Death Eaters that come after the trio (167). The difference between Ron and the Death Eaters is that Ron feels relieved when Harry says they shouldn't kill the Death Eaters, instead of following through. He didn't really want to do it. And after Fred's death, Ron yells that he wants to kill Death Eaters while shaking from rage and from grief (640). Ron wants to hurt the people who've hurt someone he loves. Wars are fought for this impulse—hurt someone else because they have hurt you, because they *will* hurt you, because they *might* hurt you. Ron's motives are unquestionably better than the Death Eaters'. But still, the impulse to kill is there.

I do not know what the right answer is. The series raises deep questions on morality. Who gets to decide between right and wrong? How do we decide who lives and who dies? And how do we figure out whose hurt is most justified? Evil in our lives needs to be confronted and not ignored, but how can we say we stand for good if we meet evil with another kind of evil? Many still believe in the old argument about taking an eye for an eye, but what have we gained if we're willing to harm someone as much as they were willing to harm us? Even if Ron kills many Death Eaters, Fred will still be gone.

⚡⚡⚡

One of the hardest lessons Harry (and we, the readers) have to learn is that Dumbledore himself is not as purely good as he might seem. When Harry discovers Dumbledore has lied to him repeatedly over the course of the books—never quite telling him the whole truth about his own life, it nearly destroys Harry. He's always depended on Dumbledore to save him in a way he's never been able to depend on anyone else.

Dumbledore is his most trusted advisor, the one who always explains to him what's going on, the one who assures him that he is still good, that he has done well. Yet, Dumbledore's struggle with good and evil is different from Harry's. While Harry struggles with rage and anger, Dumbledore's struggle is more like Voldemort's—to resist the temptation of power.

Early on in his life, Dumbledore and Grindelwald become friends and try to justify the dominion of wizards and witches over Muggles because it's for the Muggles' own good: "...That power gives us the right to rule, but it also gives us responsibilities over the ruled" (*Deathly Hallows,* 357). "For the greater good" eventually becomes Grindelwald's slogan, and he uses it as justification for all the harm he commits later. Dumbledore resented the fact that, after his parents' deaths, he needed to stay home and care for his two younger siblings. The idea of becoming a more visible, powerful, and wanted individual was seductive: "You cannot imagine how his ideas caught me, Harry, inflamed me. Muggles forced into subservience. We wizards triumphant. Grindelwald and I, the glorious young leaders of the revolution...I assuaged my conscience with empty words" (716).

I'm not sure if we can forgive Dumbledore these things. What if all of Dumbledore's later good in his life is a response to try and erase his early evil? Does it matter? Do we redeem Dumbledore the same way he offers redemption to Tom Riddle and to Snape? But perhaps it doesn't matter and Dumbledore doesn't need forgiveness. Perhaps it's enough that, later in life, he refused to let himself stay the way he had been before. He took his shame and his potential for harm and transformed it into something good, something that acts as a torch that

Harry and his followers will carry forward with them for light when they need it.

Perhaps no one is as imperfectly good as Harry himself. The bit of Voldemort within Harry is a symbol for the bit of evil that lays dormant in all of us. Harry has to fight his darker tendencies—including feelings of intense rage, hatred, or revenge—over and over, and decide which parts of himself he wants to listen to. In *Prisoner of Azkaban*, he imagines killing Sirius (before he discovers his innocence) (339). He pulls his wand on Sirius, and when Crookshanks the cat jumps up to protect Sirius, Harry casually contemplates killing them both: "So what if he had to kill the cat too? If it was prepared to die, trying to protect Black, that wasn't Harry's business" (342). In *Goblet of Fire*, he imagines using the Cruciatus Curse on Snape (300). In *Order of the Phoenix*, he pulls his wand on Dudley with "14 years' hatred...pounding in his veins" (15). After he's told Hedwig to peck Ron and Hermione until they write him letters with decent information, he's confronted with their bloodied hands, and finds he's "not at all sorry" (63). Later, when Ron is made prefect, the thought occurs to Harry that Ron must have something he, Harry, doesn't, and then he laughs at this thought, as though that couldn't possibly be true (167). After Sirius has died, Harry screams in his grief and pain that he wants to kill Bellatrix (809). And in *Deathly Hallows*, when Harry becomes obsessed with the idea of joining the Hallows, he's so focused on them that he forgets that his friend Luna Lovegood has been taken hostage (434–35).

We are all capable of being our worst selves. But Harry's decision to reject the Deathly Hallows is his rejection of his inner evil—an echo of his rejection of the Sorcerer's Stone back at the beginning of his journey. Like all of us, he'll have to keep facing this challenge again and again, but we can learn from Harry to recognize and fight the evil within ourselves. But this fight is worth it, even when it seems difficult or insignificant. Like Harry and Dumbledore show us, rejecting the evil within ourselves allows us to better challenge the evils around us.

Someone or something like Voldemort will rise again in our lives or within ourselves. But the lesson we can learn from the magical, extraordinary witches and wizards in *Harry Potter* is that they aren't always magical and extraordinary. They are as flawed and as ordinary as we've often felt. Harry is the perfect hero because he's imperfect. He's not pure good. He makes mistakes. He needs the people around him to help him do better. He's failed many times and gotten back up many more. Like Harry and Voldemort are joined together by the Horcruxes, the fact is, we are bound to life and to each other through our evil and our goodness. The fact is, we are all both good and evil. The end of the series is all the more beautiful because, despite the fact that we're not always the good people we want to be, we still manage to fight back evil, one small fist retracted each time; in the end, just as surely as evil will return, good will follow right behind.

SPECIALIS REVELIO: ON FATE AND FREE WILL

⚡⚡⚡

Choices are hard for me. The big ones—what to do with my life, what kind of person to be—yes, of course, those are difficult. But I struggle equally with the smallest choices. When hosting a party, I've secretly cried about what pizza toppings to order for everyone. One person is a vegetarian, but someone else hates vegetables, but I want only pepperoni, and aren't pizzas too expensive or unhealthy, anyway?

You'd think, then, that I'd be someone for whom astrology or religion or fate would be appealing. But I'm not. I don't believe in astrology. I don't believe in soulmates, and I don't believe things are *destined* to work out one way or another. I tend to think the world is chaos and we live our lives trying to find patterns that don't exist. I wonder if this is a kind of extreme version of a Midwest sensibility: Work hard, be practical, and things will work out—and tell yourself that anything else is a waste of speculation.

When I graduated from college, I knew I wanted to get a job as an editor. I got the job, but as soon as I did, I realized that I hadn't ever thought past that first role. It turns out that not believing in predestination and also being paralyzed with indecision means that you're not so good at creating dreams for yourself. It's easier to avoid being let down if your dreams about your fate stay small and achievable. If you don't bother to make real choices for yourself, you can never make a wrong one.

In *Harry Potter*, *Specialis Revelio* is the spell used to reveal charms or hexes. What if *Specialis Revelio* could reveal other things, like our fates and future? If we Muggles could cast *Specialis Revelio* into our futures and reveal what's ahead, would we? Is it better to know where you're going, or to discover it along the way?

In the novels, Harry is constantly dragged between the two poles of fate and free will. Is he The Chosen One, whose only living purpose is to kill Voldemort? Or is he driven instead by the choices he makes? Harry's grappling with this question is the same type we all do in our own lives: Are our futures predetermined? Does fate guide us to where we're supposed to be? Or do we make our own lives? What does it mean for us if nothing is set in stone?

As soon as Harry is born, his life is surrounded by the specter of fate, of a predetermined life. Before Harry's birth, Professor Sybill Trelawney made a prophecy: "The one with the power to vanquish the Dark Lord approaches [...] and the Dark Lord will mark him as his equal, but he will have power the Dark Lord knows not... and either must die at the hand of the other for neither can live while the other survives..."[1] (*Order of the Phoenix,* 841). Voldemort, following the prophecy, tracks Harry down, kills his parents, and unsuccessfully tries to kill Harry. From infancy, Harry's life is literally marked by fate: As a result of Voldemort's belief in prophecy, Harry is left with his lightning bolt scar and a legacy of his parents' sacrifice.

At first read, it seems like Harry is just a figurehead for those who manipulate him. In fact, both Voldemort *and* Dumbledore make the prophecy about Harry one of their main focuses. Dumbledore, in fact, works to structure Harry's life so that he grows up to fulfill his part of the prophecy. He controls what he tells Harry and when, making Harry a symbol for the influence of fate in the larger story of good versus evil.

But, of course, fate is not that simple. As tempting as it might be to have all our difficult choices predetermined and taken away from us, most of us would rather not live as actors in someone else's play. We want to own our own lives. We want to own what happens to us. As Dumbledore says in *Chamber of Secrets,* "It is our choices, Harry, that show what we truly are, far more than our abilities" (333). And Harry can teach us that although his actions appear to be controlled by fate, he is the ultimate guide of his own life.

Throughout his time at school, Harry is continually drawn into the fray and closer to Voldemort, whether he likes it or not. During the Triwizard Tournament in their fourth year, Harry is too young to compete, and he looks forward to observing the tournament as a spectator, for once, rather than as the center of attention. However, due to Barty Crouch Jr.'s meddling on

---

1   Bracketed sections replace original text.

Voldemort's behalf, Harry is drawn into the action once again. But ultimately, Harry chooses to grab the Triwizard Cup with Cedric, thus setting his own destiny in motion. (This chain of events allows Voldemort to take some of Harry's blood, which is later what saves Harry's life.)

You could argue that Voldemort wanted Harry to take the cup either way, making Harry a victim of fate or someone else's power. But that doesn't matter. In their second year, he *chooses* to help Ginny in the Chamber of Secrets. He *chooses* to go with Hermione and help free Buckbeak and Sirius in *Prisoner of Azkaban*—all of which lead him closer to Lord Voldemort. Yes, he is moving toward the prophecy, but doing so under his own power. The important thing is that Harry *chooses* to take a path of fairness and goodness. Even if they sometimes align with the prophecy, Harry's choices make him who he is, and his character is what ends up making all the difference.

And even after the prophecy is in play, Harry's life continues to be driven by his own choices, rather than by the prophecy. He doubts his position, of course—he feels like he's making choices because he *must*, because the prophecy's told him the way he must go. And yes, Harry must kill Voldemort. But not because of the prophecy. His actions feel loaded after he discovers the prophecy, to be sure, but overall, his motives have hardly changed. He wants to fight Voldemort not because of the prophecy, but because he's always wanted to fight Voldemort. Dumbledore tells Harry so: "The prophecy does not mean you *have* to do anything! In order words, you are free to choose your way, quite free to turn your back on the prophecy" (*Half-Blood Prince*, 512). Harry could have made a different choice and went into hiding somewhere. But the point is that Harry doesn't turn his back.

Although Harry appears to fulfill the prophecy in the end, that doesn't ultimately matter. It's possible that Voldemort might've gone after the Potters anyway, as they were Order of the Phoenix members and magically talented. And Harry would've gone after Voldemort no matter what. Though the prophecy does end up fulfilled, the prophecy becomes irrelevant if Harry would have fulfilled it anyway because of who he is.

Harry's personality is determined by the choices he makes, rather than by the prophecy. He chooses to ask Molly Weasley for help getting onto Platform 9¾ for the first time, which leads him to meeting Ron and Hermione on the Hogwarts Express. He chooses to turn away from the Elder Wand and the Deathly Hallows. He chooses to trust Dumbledore's Army (D.A.) and Neville to destroy the Horcruxes. He chooses to sacrifice himself. In the end, the great victory over evil is not because he was fated to win, but because his choices led him there.

And what about Neville, the Boy Who Could Have Been? Harry fantasizes about this possibility several times—what if Neville had been killed, and Harry got to kiss his own mother goodbye on Platform 9¾? However, Neville wasn't killed. The prophecy, even though it points at a kind of predestined path, is vague and could imply many different outcomes. Perhaps fate is not so fated after all. It's significant that, in their fifth year, Neville is the one who destroys (if accidentally) the prophecy in the Department of Mysteries. It's as if Neville is severing its influence on both Harry and himself. And although the longest book in the series, *Order of the Phoenix*, is mostly about the prophecy, we end the book with the prophecy destroyed.

This discovery that you must direct your own life is an unpleasant one. The responsibility of making choices is both a kind of freedom and a kind of prison. Harry confronts this realization in *Deathly Hallows*, when he finally must forge his own path. Every day, he must decide what to do next. It's no wonder that, for most of the series, Harry turns toward fate first.

Harry's curiosity about fate emerges in *Prisoner of Azkaban* with the reappearing giant black dog. He begins to look for patterns and starts to consider it an omen. In Trelawney's Divination class, he finally has a name for this creature who appears right before misfortune: the Grim. Harry starts seeing the Grim everywhere and starts to believe he might be destined for death. His desire for seeing his life as fated grows—after overhearing Sirius Black's history in the Three Broomsticks, Harry starts to believe he *must* kill Sirius Black, as a kind of karmic retribution for his parents' deaths.

Nearly everyone around Harry scoffs at the idea of omens— Divination and Professor Trelawney are widely seen as frauds, and almost no one takes her predictions seriously (except for Lavender and Parvati, who are portrayed as gullible fangirls). But a careful reader will note that nearly every single one of Trelawney's predictions do come true (except, ironically, guessing Harry's birth month). In addition to the prophecy about Voldemort and Wormtail returning, her smaller predictions are just as accurate. In the first Divination class, Trelawney predicts Neville will break his teacup. Minutes later, he does. In *Goblet of Fire*, she says to Harry, "I fear the thing you dread will indeed come to pass" (199)—and *many* things Harry dreads will indeed come to pass, including the loss of his father figures Sirius and Dumbledore, his friends doubting him, and his own brush with death. In *Goblet of Fire*, Professor Trelawney sees death "com[ing], ever closer, it circles overhead like a vulture, ever lower...ever lower over the castle..." (372). There's much eye-rolling, of course, but Cedric's death waits ahead of them. And in *Half-Blood Prince*, Trelawney says she sees the "lightning-struck tower...calamity. Disaster" (543). And of course, later in the book, Dumbledore dies at the top of Hogwarts's tallest tower. Firenze, the centaur, mentions the brightness of Mars—the planet associated with war—after Voldemort's return in *Order of the Phoenix*, foreshadowing the Battle of Hogwarts: "Mars, bringer of battle, shines brightly above us, suggesting that the fight must break out again soon" (603).

This accuracy does seem to point toward the influence of fate (and it certainly points to the fact that Trelawney deserves much more respect than she gets, despite her dottiness). But, frankly, most of Harry's life has been grim. If it feels like the Grim foretells misfortune, well, what else can happen to Harry but unfortunate things? It's surprising he's only beginning to see the Grim at that point in time. And even when we later find out that the Grim is actually Sirius, Harry's soon-to-be-beloved godfather, you could argue that his form as a black dog is a symbol of Sirius's own tragic end.

What's the use of fate, though, if we can only see its work after it's too late? Fate can feel like an explanation for the awful things in our lives, because the awful things feel just a bit less awful if we feel like they happened on purpose. Like Harry and many others, we look for prophecy and fate to help us feel better. As Hermione says, the Grim isn't a symbol for something worse to come—the fear of the Grim scares people to death. We all have our own personal Grims that haunt us, and when that chaos comes, we think that we should have seen it coming all along.

However, Trelawney's and Firenze's predictions might not point to a predestined path. They might show us something far more terrifying than fate: the randomness of bad luck. Instead of fate, the arbitrary forces of luck bend life into shapes you don't recognize, and that's simply the way life works. Sometimes our lives are linear and beautiful and logical, but often they are not. Life shows us symmetry just as often as it shows us chaos. The things we worry about are rarely the things that happen. Instead, unimaginable terrible things find us. Terrible things happen when they're least convenient. They often do not lead to a larger understanding or a clearer path, but instead leave our futures as fogged as an unyielding crystal ball.

Perhaps the pull of fate versus free will does not have to be one thing or the other. Life is a combination of "fate"—whatever you want to call fate—and free will. As much as we'd like to predict what's coming, we'll never be able to predict anything aside from the fact that, indeed, both good and bad things will happen to us.

Our choices can help us make our own destiny, but they cannot keep us from the broken teacups and Grims in our paths. When Harry chooses not to kill Pettigrew in *Prisoner of Azkaban*, he sees this as a kind of domino effect for Voldemort's return (and later, Sirius's death): "I stopped Sirius and Professor Lupin from killing Pettigrew! That makes it my fault if Voldemort comes back!" (426). Dumbledore won't let Harry blame himself. As he says, there are too many variables and too much chaos to blame ourselves for what happens to us: "The consequences of our actions are always so complicated, so diverse, that predicting the future is a very difficult business indeed.... You did a very noble thing, in saving Pettigrew's life'" (426). Yes, Pettigrew's freedom leads to Voldemort's return and Voldemort's return leads to Sirius's death. But Harry's choice to spare Pettigrew ultimately leads to Pettigrew's act of mercy in *Deathly Hallows*, his silver hand releasing its grip on Harry's neck to save Harry's life. And Harry is a better person for not having murdered Pettigrew, even if Pettigrew deserved it. As Slughorn says, "Killing rips the soul apart" (*Half-Blood Prince*, 498), and as a result of his choices, Harry's soul remains intact. Though Harry feels like his choice was the wrong one, he'll discover that his choices led him to a better version of himself and allowed him to continue on in his chosen fight. Fate's influence, along with our own choices, gives us the chance to learn and to experience both sweet and sour. We can never know how our actions will turn out, so we must do the best we can.

As much as we're able, we want to choose where we're headed. The world may lay out paths that we didn't expect, but ultimately we choose what we want to do. Which path do we want to take—Hallows or Horcruxes? Do we sit down and refuse to go? Do we walk? Do we run? We make a choice, and we make our own destiny. Instead of seeing Trelawney's predictions as a kind of fated path, I've started reading them as potential. Instead of letting the unexpected chaos of life overwhelm us, or choosing to avoid choice altogether, upheaval can create new paths ahead of us. It's up to us whether we want to see them, or which way we want to go.

EVANESCO: ON LOSING OUR HEROES

As a child, I saw my grandfather as a kind of superhero. He wasn't someone I wanted to be, necessarily, but he was someone whose bravery and whose stories I wanted to absorb. He'd parachuted out of planes, he'd raced cars, he'd even punched someone so hard they flew off the porch and landed in the dirt. He'd broken both his arms and his legs when his parachute failed, and he lived. He'd wrecked a race car so badly it was a flattened metal pancake, and he walked out alive. He's 82 and he still walks without a cane or walker. In my mind, my grandfather always strolled in the eye of a storm, flicking away a cigarette (he's been smoking since he was nine years old), unafraid.

As I've grown up, I've had to relearn who my grandfather is. His life has been incredible, certainly, and he's behaved heroically many times, but many of these stories are exaggerated, more beautiful and violent than they were in real life, the way all stories are. My grandfather has been many things, but he is also a regular man. He lost his first wife to breast cancer. He wears a hearing aid. He loves steak and potatoes, though he knows he should eat less of them. The older we get, the more frequently we have to face the fact that writers or actors or teachers or other people we love, in our lives and from afar, are not always as heroic as they appear. Growing up means facing the fact that those we look up to, while worthy of our gaze, are often equally as unworthy—just as human and fallible as anyone. Growing up can feel like your heroes begin to fall around you, leaving you standing alone. But that loss doesn't have to leave us bereft—instead, we can redefine the terms of being a hero and find ourselves again, not standing below or behind perfect people forever ahead of us, untouchable, but standing beside them, shoulder to shoulder.

⚡⚡⚡

Heroes are thick on the ground of the *Harry Potter* series. From the moment Harry enters the wizarding world, he's confronted with a long legacy of heroes he's never had—the professors at Hogwarts who seem to have existed there forever; the old witches and wizards that wave at him from Chocolate Frog cards; and of course, Dumbledore. Growing up, Harry had no opportunity for heroes. His parents, his only chance for someone to look up to, are vague memories, who allegedly died unheroic and average in a car crash. It's no surprise that Harry (and the readers) immediately looks to Dumbledore as a hero, his reverence helped along by Ron's frank admiration on their first Hogwarts Express trip. But who wouldn't see Dumbledore this way? Old, twinkly, magnificently bearded— Dumbledore is the most perfect grandfather figure any of us could imagine. We love Dumbledore as much as Harry does. Though an old man, he shows no evidence of senility or weakness. He is like your grandfather at both his most wise and most powerful moments. We are drawn to Dumbledore the way we all are with our heroes, the way a leaf is swept into a current—head-on, with nothing to do but let yourself be pulled along.

Once Harry learns the real story of his parents' deaths, they become the heroes he's always wanted. Just like Dumbledore is heroic perfection, so, too, are his parents: a happy young couple, a talented witch and wizard, Voldemort resistance-fighters, universally beloved, with a young son they gave their lives for. Reveling in their legacy allows Harry a small bit of the childhood with them he never got to have; he pictures his parents as providers, protectors, unblemished in their complete love for him. And Harry's relationship to his parents is even purer than ours might have been as children—since he's lost both of them already, he doesn't even have the privilege that children in loving homes have: taking their parents for granted.

Too soon, though, Harry must face the fact that his heroes are not who he thought they were. The current that swept him up slows, and he's left without a push or direction. This is part of the difficulty of growing up: We lose our parents. Not in that final, inevitable way; rather, we lose the parents we had as children. We have to meet our parents all over again as adults, their lives a bright hallway we've never visited, much longer and more complex than ours, alien from and similar to ours in ways we might never be able to understand.

Harry resists this knowledge, of course. It hurts to lose the parents you thought you had, especially when they are the pristine, uncomplicated ones we are lucky to have as children. For Harry, this loss is even more profound; right after he's learned the true, heroic story of their deaths and built a careful monument to them within himself, he must lose his parents a second time. For many years, he ignores Snape's snide comments about James Potter and Sirius Black, assuming that Snape is just bitter or jealous and that his words can't possibly be true. But after a visit to the Pensieve, he learns that 15-year-old James and Sirius sometimes *were* cruel and arrogant, as 15-year-olds can be, and he's forced to face his father and Sirius without the glow of heroism for the first time: "Whenever someone had told him he was like James, he had glowed with pride inside. And now...he felt cold and miserable at the thought of him" (*Order of the Phoenix*, 650).

Though this new information about Harry's heroes means he must face them more fully, more painfully, this loss also gives him new insight. This moment of discovering James's and Sirius's humanity gives Harry something he's never allowed himself before: empathy with Snape. Seeing Snape bullied, Harry "knew exactly how it felt to be humiliated in the middle of a circle of onlookers, knew exactly how Snape had felt..." (650).

In light of this discovery, James becomes a different kind of hero to Harry, but this awareness allows Harry to gain a new hero in Snape, albeit gradually. Snape's heroism is, though flawed and cruel in its own way, built on the same sacrifice Harry's parents made. He gives himself up so that Harry can be saved. And in the end, Harry recognizes the sacrifice as heroic: He gives his son Snape's name, so that the younger Albus Severus Potter will feel the weight of the imperfect heroes whose names he's been given when he goes to Hogwarts. And young Albus will also inevitably have to reckon with his father's legacy as The Chosen One.

Dumbledore takes much longer to fall as Harry's hero than his parents and Sirius do. Since Harry has been able to physically go to Dumbledore with his worries, to watch Dumbledore in power and to physically feel Dumbledore's protection over him (the way he couldn't with his parents), it is more difficult for Harry to let him go. Dumbledore's presence is a continual comfort for Harry. In *Goblet of Fire*, when Harry starts seeing inside Voldemort's mind, he goes to see Dumbledore. It's not until he sits in Dumbledore's office that he feels calm. The space itself is a comfort (582). When Harry has to go to a hearing in *Order of the Phoenix*, Dumbledore shows up in Harry's defense to save him—and in the terrifying courtroom, he provides a literal sense of comfort: two squashy armchairs (139).

Dumbledore is a hero in many ways. He's a defender of Muggles and house-elf and goblin rights, and the winner of the duel with Grindelwald. But much of Harry's sense of Dumbledore's heroism is a fantasy. Even as early as *Prisoner of Azkaban*, Harry starts to worry that Dumbledore might not always be there for him in the way he might want, such as when Harry's trying to save Sirius from being wrongly executed: "Harry stared up into [Dumbledore's] grave face and felt as though the ground beneath him were falling sharply away. He had grown used to the idea that Dumbledore could solve anything. He had expected Dumbledore to pull some amazing solution out of the air. But no...their last hope was gone" (393). Of course, Dumbledore does come up with the solution of the Time Turner, but he expects Harry and Hermione to do this work themselves.

Even in *Sorcerer's Stone* and *Chamber of Secrets*, Dumbledore isn't present in the most dangerous moments. He's present to explain things, after the fact, but for the most part, Harry and the trio are on their own. When, in *Order of the Phoenix*, Dumbledore arrives at the Ministry, Harry feels relief as fierce as electricity "through every particle of his body—they were saved" (805). But even so, Dumbledore is not able to save Sirius, Harry's only other living hero. Dumbledore arrives, but he ultimately cannot protect Harry from hurt. Dumbledore is a source of history and knowledge, and does save their lives a time or two, but Harry's sense of him as a hero is largely invented out of his own intense need for one.

This chapter is named for *Evanesco*, the spell that causes things to disappear. And inevitably, the way we all must, Harry loses his hero. Not once, but twice. First, when Dumbledore dies, that comfort he provided is abruptly gone. And by the time we reach the *Deathly Hallows*, Harry loses Dumbledore when he begins to learn about Dumbledore's life before they met. The more Harry learns about Dumbledore's past—his affiliation with Grindelwald, the concept of "for the greater good," the idea of wizard dominance over Muggles and other creatures, Dumbledore's leaving his family and his sister's death—the more Harry loses the hero he thought he had. The readers, too, must confront their own assumptions about Dumbledore and realize that, however good and powerful he was, our hero was also a regular man: flawed, capable of making mistakes.

He was wise and kind, yet he still lets Harry down and he lets us down, as well.

And as the books progress, Harry is more and more able to come to terms with his own lack of true heroes. In *Order of the Phoenix*, when he sees the vision of Sirius hurt at the Ministry, McGonagall is gone, Dumbledore and Hagrid are gone, and Harry realizes "there was nobody left to tell" (730). Later, after Dumbledore's death, Harry firmly closes the door on his old ideas about heroism: Harry "must abandon forever the illusion he ought to have lost at the age of one, that the shelter of a parent's arms meant that nothing could hurt him," now that all of his adult protectors have left him (*Half-Blood Prince*, 645). Even though he has the heroic effort of his friends, his family, and Dumbledore behind him in the final chapters of *Deathly Hallows*, in the end, Harry walks alone into the forest. The ghosts of his parents, Sirius, and Lupin disappear. We all must eventually strike out alone, without our heroes.

But even when Harry goes off on his own, his heroes are still beside him, in a way. He never quite lets go of the heroic image of his parents, Sirius, or even Dumbledore; his conception of who they are as heroes just changes. He needs them differently, as he needs different kinds of heroes at different points in his life. A hero doesn't have to be someone who saves us or protects us; our heroes can instead be our teachers and our role models, the way Harry calls his parents up with the Resurrection Stone as he's about to sacrifice himself. They can't do anything to protect him—they are just smoke, insubstantial—but they are still present for Harry. Harry follows the path his parents cut for him: He is flawed and has struggled, but he, like his parents and like Dumbledore, is willing to sacrifice himself for others. He catches up to where his parents left off and steps in time beside them. And in *Deathly Hallows*, Harry even becomes what Dumbledore was to him—a guide, a provider of knowledge. In Chapter 24, "The Wandmaker," Harry uses his interviews with Griphook the goblin and Ollivander to teach himself about the Deathly Hallows and about the remaining Horcruxes. This chapter is the equivalent of the preceding chapters where Dumbledore explains everything. But now, at last, Harry is able to do it himself.

And that's the point, isn't it? People behave heroically, but no one is a perfect hero. Harry, as his ordinary, flawed self, is the one who steps up to do what needs to be done. He is not a hero; he is who he is through a random set of circumstances and choices. But when he chooses to sacrifice himself, he behaves heroically for a moment. Perhaps this is what we should hope for: not a superhero walking through a storm, but a chance to find an ordinary hero, doing the difficult thing when it's needed the most. Perhaps we can become like Harry, Ron, and Hermione, and we can learn to become this kind of hero ourselves, among all our ordinary days.

RENNERVATE: ON KNOWLEDGE AND LOSS OF INNOCENCE

Like most schools in mostly white middle-class America, mine gave me a brief history of slavery in the United States— emphasis on "brief." I knew what the Civil War was, I knew why it happened, and I knew slavery had existed and that it had been bad. I knew there had been a Civil Rights Movement, and of course I knew about Dr. Martin Luther King Jr. But we were otherwise shielded from what slavery had meant, and the way that the trauma, violence, and discrimination of slavery and racism spread like cracks on glass into the present day, each injustice pressing harder, the cracked lines getting longer.

I tended to think of slavery as something that had happened long ago, and something that we were done with now. But in college, I had a professor who required us to go to the library and re-expose ourselves to the history we'd missed. We examined what segregation actually looked like in practice, the racist images in pop culture and advertisements, and the racism embedded in our legal and housing systems, like a steel frame under concrete, propping everything else up.

In Germany, there are over 2,000 Holocaust memorial sites. And yet, in the United States, where over 4,000 people were lynched, we don't have any kind of prominent memorial. We White Americans pretend that slavery was just an aberration, some kind of mistake, and that we're done with that. We prefer to not remember it.

Not remembering it means not learning from it. It means erasing everything that happened, and erasing the people it happened to. We do children a disservice by hiding this knowledge from them. We might be trying to preserve their innocence, but the fact is that many children have already had their innocence taken away by a racist history. We would do better to give everyone the knowledge of the truth.

The Equal Justice Initiative (EJI) is an organization that is planning to build a Lynching Memorial, to do what Germany has been doing for years; to face the pain of their past, gain the knowledge, and do our own work to move forward. Like the spell *Rennervate*, we have a chance to revive and reawaken a truer version of the past. EJI director Bryan Stevenson has argued that "our nation's history of racial injustice casts a shadow across the American landscape. This shadow cannot be lifted until we shine the light of truth on the destructive violence that shaped our nation."[2] Even though knowledge means we must reshape what we knew and who we were

2 "The Memorial to Peace and Justice," Equal Justice Initiative, 2017, http://eji.org/national-lynching-memorial, accessed 10 June 2017.

before, the truth is necessary if it means we can learn and do better next time.

$$\lightning\ \lightning\ \lightning$$

One of the biggest journeys of Harry's life is the one he takes within—the journey from ignorance and innocence to new knowledge—knowledge about his family, himself, and mortality. He starts the series in a place of confusion, asking, why do these things happen to him? Why is his past such a locked door? Why is knowledge kept from him? Why is the cupboard under the stairs his life? But with his first owl post and with Hagrid come the biggest piece of knowledge of his life: He's a wizard. This knowledge is a gift. It answers so many of the questions he's held for so long, and, like most knowledge does, it gives him a kind of access. With the knowledge that he's a wizard, Harry gets to join the world where he finally belongs. Harry's life is cleaved in half—who he was before he knew he was a wizard, and who he could now become.

In many ways, his new knowledge means he has to start all over again, at Hogwarts. The first three books are beautiful for us, the readers, as we get to experience the joy of new knowledge with Harry—opening his vault at Gringotts (a physical reminder of his parents' care for him) getting a wand at Ollivander's, the ghosts and the dormitory and the moving staircases and magical classes at Hogwarts. *Sorcerer's Stone* through *Prisoner of Azkaban* feel like those first days of school before you learn to dread it, where you experience the excitement of new pencils, of seeing your friends again or deciding whether that boy you liked is even cuter now, of new classes and new spaces. Early, innocent knowledge feels simple and linear. Like Harry, it's through knowledge that we're able to try and discover who we are.

In the first three books, though, Harry and the trio's knowledge is often the incomplete knowledge of children. It's easy to forget that they are children, since we're in their minds and we remember what it's like to feel 11, 12, and 13, to feel like you're grown up, but to also feel that it's frustratingly unfair that the grownups around you don't believe or can't tell that you're a grownup, too, and withhold things that you'd like to know. It's this incomplete knowledge that makes them confident and bold—they (well, Harry and Ron, at least) don't feel many qualms about confronting a troll, or trying to get past Fluffy the three-headed dog, or about sliding down a tube into a secret passageway into who-knows-where to try and rescue Ginny. Despite their initial terror when they first find Fluffy in *The Sorcerer's Stone,* by the next morning, Harry and Ron think "that meeting the three-headed dog had been an excellent adventure, and they were quite keen to have another one" (163).

From young Harry and Ron, we can remind ourselves when our children or our young family members or friends do stupid things that might hurt them, they're working on learning. They're testing the incomplete knowledge they have. We can try to remember what it felt like to think that you knew everything by reflecting on our own past actions. In *Prisoner of Azkaban,* when Harry seems impressed by Professor Lupin's stories about the adventures of Moony, Padfoot, Prongs, and Wormtail, adventures that easily could have gotten them killed, Lupin cautions Harry, "...there were near misses, many of them. We laughed about them afterwards. We were young, thoughtless—carried away with our own cleverness" (355).

But as Harry gets older and learns more about his own family, about Voldemort, about Dumbledore, and about himself, his exposure to knowledge raises as many questions as it answers. As Harry gains more and more knowledge about the wizarding world, he's forced to keep reckoning with how much he has left to discover. This is why the first two books feel slightly lighter than the rest. Harry's knowledge is still building, rather than forcing him to break down and rebuild again. But once Sirius enters the story, Harry must start to confront the things he thought he knew about himself and about his parents. The story deepens and gets darker the more Harry learns who he is. We realize that knowledge can be disruptive. Sometimes knowledge can leave us less certain than when we started. Each time we learn something, we move a bit further from the place we were as children, when we were innocent and unaware.

The person in the series who understands knowledge the least is, unfortunately, a professor: Umbridge. (Though, to call her a professor is perhaps an insult to real professors.) She tries to force a kind of stupidity on the students, even when they are interested in learning more about how to work defensive spells in the real world. When Harry points out that reading silently from a book is not likely to be super helpful when they're attacked by Voldemort, Umbridge responds, "This is school, Mr. Potter, not the real world" (*Order of the Phoenix,* 244). She repeatedly puts her students down and insinuates that people around her are incompetent or stupid.

Despite her efforts not to, Umbridge can still teach us something. She can teach us that our knowledge will always need to be adapted so it can live in the real world. And even though Umbridge unfortunately ends up with some power at the Ministry, her ideas don't last, thanks to Hermione and Fred and George's ouster of Umbridge from Hogwarts. We can learn that the ignorant can convince some people of their ideas, but not everyone, and not for long. From Fred and George, and all the other students who defy Umbridge, we can learn to be brave enough to be our own educators in the face of people who tell us that we're not capable.

As we get older, knowledge can become partly a recognition of your own lack of knowledge, of uncertainty. One of the hardest and most valuable things you'll ever learn is that you don't know what you're doing. And even more than that, you learn that no one else around you knows what they're doing. Part of growing up is understanding that you *don't* know everything— no one knows everything. We see this transition happen with Harry, Ron, and Hermione. When they were kids, they were more confident, but as Harry grows up he seems to understand how much luck is at play in his life, and how much everyone is just winging it. Hermione, too, is forced to confront the fact that she might not know everything: When she's trying to help Harry with the second task in *Goblet of Fire*, she, of course, spends time in the library, but with no success. In that moment, Hermione "seemed to be taking the library's lack of useful information on the subject as a personal insult; it had never failed her before" (486). Understanding that you don't know everything isn't an easy process.

When, in *Order of the Phoenix*, Hermione is trying to convince Harry to form what will become Dumbledore's Army, Harry nearly refuses because his new knowledge of the world makes him doubt himself. After Hermione and Ron recount his previous successful exploits (like defeating Quirrell, the basilisk, and the Triwizard Tournament), Harry says, "...all that stuff was luck—I didn't know what I was doing half the time, I didn't plan any of it, I just did whatever I could think of, and I nearly always had help" (327). This admission, though, is what prompts Hermione to say Voldemort's name out loud for the first time (328). And this is partly why Harry agrees to start the D.A., one of the most important actions the trio takes. Hermione takes it seriously enough to use Voldemort's name, which helps Harry realize how necessary the D.A. is. She acknowledges the evil directly, rather than avoiding it. From Harry, we can learn that the same maturity it takes to admit we don't know what we're doing can also give others the courage to take action, to figure out what they're doing. By admitting we're not sure, we are also committing to doing the best we can with the knowledge we have.

And the trio must learn this lesson more than once, most painfully in *Deathly Hallows*. When the trio decides to leave Hogwarts and set out to go destroy Horcruxes on their way to defeating Voldemort, Hermione and Ron assume that Harry has some kind of secret knowledge or plan beyond what he's told them. They are like their 11-year-old selves again, charging off on Halloween to go attack a troll, without a plan, certain that everything will work out. But now that the stakes are so much higher, their tolerance for moving without a plan quickly wanes. When they arrive at yet another campsite, with nothing to show for it, Ron yells at Harry, "We thought you knew what you were doing!" (307). And this confirms Harry's greatest fear—that Ron and Hermione will consider his lack of knowledge a fault, and consider him a fraud, rather than standing beside him. He starts to doubt their motives, their mission, and himself: "...they were three teenagers in a tent whose only achievement was not, yet, to be dead" (308). Like Harry, we must face our own lack of knowledge again and again. Sometimes, we have to learn to move forward despite our uncertainty. The only thing to do is to blunder on.

Even as we gain new knowledge, or acknowledge everything we still have left to learn, our old knowledge can still serve us. When Harry is in the graveyard crouching behind a gravestone and waiting to be murdered by Voldemort in *Goblet of Fire*, he's racking his brains to try to figure out what to do. He feels the way we've all felt in front of something that terrifies us—that we've wasted our chance to prepare, that we haven't done enough, and that we're utterly unequipped for this moment. He flashes back to Defense Against the Dark Arts professor Gilderoy Lockhart's dueling club and all the nothing he learned there. In that moment, his *Expelliarmus*, his only weapon, feels like nothing.

But, as we know, that simple spell he learned, even from useless Lockhart, is what saves him. With his memory of the small, seemingly paltry bit of knowledge he obtained as a 12-year-old, he creates *Priori Incantatem*, which allows him to see the ghosts of his parents. His humility in using this simple spell allows him one of the things he wants most desperately—the comfort of his parents. In our greatest moments of terror, our knowledge from our younger selves will still serve us. No matter how simple the knowledge, no matter if we feel we still have so much more to learn, no matter if we don't know what to do, our knowledge will be the buoy that keeps us from going under.

But moving forward means doing more than just floating—it means you have to start swimming. It means work. Much of the knowledge that Harry has to face hurts him deeply, and he resists it. The knowledge that his father James might sometimes have been the arrogant man Snape thought he was hurts. The knowledge that Dumbledore was not always honest with him hurts. The knowledge that without Wormtail's cowardice, he might still have parents, hurts the most. Like Barty Crouch Jr. (still in the form of Moody) says when demonstrating the Unforgivable Curses, knowledge makes you "appreciate what the worst is" (*Goblet of Fire*, 217).

For Harry, and for readers, the worst knowledge we'll have to face is the knowledge of our own mortality, and the deaths of loved ones. And Harry, sweet Harry, has to face the brutal knowledge of loss over and over again, and try to claw his way to the surface and return to himself each time. After Cedric's death and during Harry's traumatic experience in the graveyard, Voldemort puts the Imperius Curse on him. And the Imperius Curse feels good—control is taken away from you, your mind is wiped blank, empty, with no pain, no memory, nothing other than waiting to hear someone else give you instructions (*Goblet of Fire*, 661). Harry craves this release.

We see it again after Sirius's death, when Harry feels so consumed with the knowledge that he was fooled, that Sirius was lured to the Department of Mysteries because of him, that he feels he caused Sirius's death. Afterward, he sits in

Dumbledore's office in pain: "Harry could not stand this, he could not stand being Harry anymore.... He had never felt more trapped inside his own head and body, never wished so intensely that he could be somebody—anybody—else..." (*Order of the Phoenix*, 822). He later screams at Dumbledore that if pain makes him human, then he doesn't want to be human (824). His new knowledge of grief is such that he wants to leave his own body. He wants to stop existing. But eventually, he must return. In the graveyard, he shakes off Voldemort's Imperius Curse and has to face again the pain he's already experienced, and the pain that's likely ahead. One of the most moving moments of reading the series is when, in *Deathly Hallows*, the readers finally have to face the full scene of Harry's parents' deaths (342–45). We no longer get the reprieve of an interruption by scene change, or by Harry's return to consciousness, or by a joke of Fred and George's or Ron's. We have to face the completeness of their loss along with Harry, and we can no longer flinch.

In *Goblet of Fire*, Dumbledore asks Harry to relive and retell what happened, saying, "Numbing the pain for a while will make it worse when you finally feel it" (695). I'm not sure I buy this, Dumbledore. I think sometimes we *need* to numb the pain. I think we need moments like the quiet ones Harry spends out on the grounds alone after Sirius's death. If we need to numb ourselves for a while to protect our hearts, we should. And Harry does find that, once he's able to face Sirius's death directly, he feels a bit better.

Near the end of *Order of the Phoenix*, Harry talks not with Ron or Hermione, who can't understand his grief, but with Luna, who lost her mother and who can understand. When

Harry asks her about it, she acknowledges the pain right away: "Yes, it was rather horrible" (863). Her ability to face the pain helps Harry face his, and after he leaves her, "he found that the terrible weight in his stomach seemed to have lessened slightly" (864). Like the thestrals at Hogwarts, present, but temporarily invisible to some, pain has always existed; it's up to us and the ways in which we arm ourselves to see it. Harry learns this lesson when he finally gets to visit Godric's Hollow, the neighborhood he was born in but doesn't remember. When he finally finds his old family home, he learns that it's not been leveled or polished up for tourists. Instead, the house has been left a wreck. A sign in front states: "This house, invisible to Muggles, has been left in its ruined state as a monument to the Potters and as a reminder of the violence that tore apart their family" (*Deathly Hallows*, 332–33). Harry carries the violence of his parents' deaths with him, but the wizarding world (and our own) needs this explicit reminder to face its history with open eyes. We do not wish this knowledge of death and violence on anyone. We shield children from the cruelties of the world for as long as we can. But eventually, that knowledge will creep in, like salt into a wound. We must face it. When we have this kind of difficult knowledge, we can see things more clearly and brightly, the way a morning looks after a bad night of storm.

New knowledge forces self-reflection and gives us the chance to redefine ourselves again and again, our definitions getting better, sharper each time. Every piece of knowledge that Harry learns means he has to lose a bit more of his innocence, but by equal measure, he adds to his own foundation. Harry repeatedly sees these turning points in his own becoming.

He sees himself in Lockhart's dueling club "as though from a former life" (*Goblet of Fire,* 660).

When, in *Order of the Phoenix,* he stumbles on Molly Weasley trying to get rid of a boggart as it turns into the dead bodies of each of her children, of her husband, and of Harry, Harry is forced to face a new kind of knowledge for the first time: that of the very real danger they're facing, and his own mortality. At that moment, he reflects on who he had been before, and "felt older than he had ever felt in his life" (178). He's amazed that, a few hours beforehand, he'd been worrying about a prefect badge. He's replacing his old worries with newer, deeper ones. Later in *Order of the Phoenix,* after the mass Azkaban breakout, no other students seem concerned, since they don't read the news. Harry can't believe that "there they all were, talking about homework and Quidditch and who knew what other rubbish, and outside these walls 10 more Death Eaters had swollen Voldemort's ranks" (545). Harry would love to return to a blissful lack of knowledge. He'd rather be freed from it and return to innocence. But he recognizes that he needs to reckon with it.

In the final battle, when Neville carries tiny Colin Creevey's dead body, he, too, must face new knowledge: the terrible grief of innocent deaths. This knowledge changes Neville so much that Harry says, "He looked like an old man" (*Deathly Hallows,* 694). After any loss, when a person is faced with a new and terrible kind of knowledge, we can see two different parts of ourselves—who we were before, and who we've become.

Gaining knowledge is about becoming more fully who we are. Harry's old knowledge of *Expelliarmus* becomes a defining fact about who he is: someone who would always rather disarm than kill. His knowledge of the Horcruxes means he loses his childhood sense of who he is, and instead, he must face the fact that he's always been the last Horcrux, and has always carried a part of Voldemort inside him. This final realization, however painful, is what allows him to understand what he needs to do to save his community: sacrifice himself. After Bellatrix Lestrange, the witch who tortured Neville's parents into insanity, escapes from Azkaban in *Order of the Phoenix*, Neville changes dramatically, becoming more focused in the D.A. meetings, and a better wizard than he's ever been before (553). His new knowledge gives him power. And after Harry's experience in the graveyard in *Goblet of Fire*, Dumbledore tells Harry: "You have shouldered a grown wizard's burden and found yourself equal to it" (699).

Knowledge is a gift. Knowledge is access, discovery, reflection, and most of all, a form of courage to face the truth in others and in ourselves. As with Harry, our own knowledge that feels like it could break us could also be our greatest form of strength. We can learn to never stop learning, and to keep building even when it would be easier to let the house collapse. To paraphrase Hagrid at the end of *Goblet of Fire*, what will come will come, and we will have to meet it when it does. Like Harry, we can hope to pick up our hammers, shoulder our own burdens, and find ourselves equal to them.

EXPECTO PATRONUM: ON LONELINESS, FRIENDSHIP, AND COMMUNITY

For this chapter I went looking for the best, most ultimate story of a friendship. I wanted to find friends who'd saved each other's lives, like Harry, Ron, and Hermione have done. I wanted people giving up organs, splitting themselves open for their friends. I wanted people stepping in front of bullets for their friends. I wanted high-drama, earth-shattering friendship.

And I did find some: At a high school in Pittsburg, when Alex Hriba came to school armed with two kitchen knives, two best friends saved each other's lives. Brett jumped in front of his friend Grace and took a knife for her, and she put pressure on his wound until the paramedics arrived.[3] I found stories of veterans who survived the trenches. I heard stories

3 "Best friends who saved each other's lives in Franklin Regional stabbing reunited." WPXI-TV News. 10 April 2014. Cox Media Group. wpxi.com/news/local/stabbing-victim-talks-about-saving-classmates-life/139547045#. Accessed 10 June 2017.

of people finding Internet friends who talked them through depression when no one in their real lives would. I heard of friends sitting in hospitals with each other, driving across the country for each other. Literature, too, is filled with these do-or-die friendships.

But sometimes more important than those big, dramatic moments are the smaller, everyday moments of friendship. They are like Ron's arm around Hermione. They are like Hermione wrapping up toast for Harry when he doesn't want to face Ron or the attention of the Great Hall, but still needs to eat. They are like my group of friends from high school and our long WhatsApp thread, where we can reach out at any time and one of the five of us knows to ask if the other is okay.

A study in Australia showed that older people with larger groups of friends were 22% less likely to die during the course of the study. Another study showed that women with breast cancer with few friends were four times as likely to die as those women with 10 or more friends—even our bodies tell us that we need our friends to survive. It didn't even matter whether the friends were nearby or not—proximity wasn't a factor. And in 2008, researchers conducted a study where students were asked to stand at the base of a steep hill with a heavy backpack. Some students stood next to friends, and others stood alone. Then they were asked to estimate the steepness of the hill. Researchers found that "the students who stood with friends gave lower estimates of the steepness of the hill. And the longer the friends had known each other, the less steep the hill appeared." The point is that friendship is measured not just in those moments of peril, but in those small moments, like when getting ready to climb hills, too.[4]

$$ \text{⚡⚡⚡} $$

The best friend I've managed to keep for the longest time is my sister. We live on opposite sides of the country now, but since we were kids, we've been close enough to read each other's minds. I trust her to support me like I trust very few others. If I had to use *Expecto Patronum* and produce a Patronus, the charm to protect from the cold of Dementors (or their analogy—depression), I know thinking of our friendship would help me do it.

Reading *Harry Potter*, we feel both the joy and sometimes the pain of friendships. Many of us have had many best friends, but will lose many best friends, too. And it's not always from a catastrophic loss, like from an accident or a fight, but often a slower, less noticeable loss, like the way light fades at the end of the day. You notice the light going, but then you look up and it's become night, and you missed the moment it happened. You couldn't find that exact moment, even if you tried. It's no one's fault but time and distance.

Harry feels it when Ron and Hermione leave to go to the prefect's carriage for the first time in *Order of the Phoenix*. He feels "an odd sense of loss. He had never traveled on the Hogwarts Express without Ron" (184). And just a bit later, when they get to Hogsmeade station, for the first time, Hagrid

---

4   Parker-Pope, Tara. "What Are Friends For?: A Longer Life." *New York Times.* 20 April 2009. nytimes.com/2009/04/21/health/21well .html. Accessed 10 June 2017.

isn't there to greet him (197). In the silence without him, Harry has to grow up and go on alone. This slow separation is the way friendships can begin to fade as we grow up.

But Harry and his friends manage to resist that fade. The friendship between Harry, Ron, and Hermione is one of the best love stories in the series. They pull together the way friends do when you're young—out of proximity, out of agreeing about something, out of not wanting to sit by yourself at lunch. They are friends shoved together by chance, by choosing to offer a small kindness to each other: a seat in the same compartment and a conversation about a missing toad. But their friendship grows and evolves beyond their chance meeting into questions of love and loyalty. And like so many great loves, the trio continues to choose each other.

Despite the ever-present fact of the trio's tight friendship, all three experience loneliness in some form or another, and this loneliness is part of what continues to bond them together. Even though far more people will know Harry's name than Ron or Hermione's, Harry is, at his core, lonely. He has the loneliness of an orphan—no matter how many friends he makes or how much Molly or Ginny Weasley love him, he will still always be without parents. And since he lost them when he was a baby, he doesn't even have memories to hold to. His loneliness stems from the fact that he never had his parents to begin with.

His path and journey in life is a lonely one, too. Because no one else has ever survived the killing curse, no one can ever understand what he's gone through. And though he doesn't know it, he's also a Horcrux. He'll never meet someone truly like him, and that's a deep kind of loneliness. Still, his is a loneliness we're all familiar with, even if we're not The Chosen One and not hacking a truly new path through life's undergrowth. Even the people closest to us, even the people that know us so well they can anticipate what we need before we do, will never be able to feel exactly what it's like to be us. Perhaps this is why Harry is often furious or despondent at being left out, especially during *Order of the Phoenix*—it's what he's felt his whole life. Harry is all of us when we feel excluded and forgotten. And that is why the trio is so important to him. Their friendship is a kind of shield against the loneliness he carries.

Ron, too, feels loneliness. Though he's the opposite of Harry, with a huge family support system, he doesn't feel as connected or wanted as the rest of his siblings might. He feels overshadowed by Charlie and Bill's interesting, older lives; Percy's ambition; and Fred and George's popularity. And he's frequently alone, too, despite all the people in his house. Charlie and Bill are no longer at home, Percy deserts the family, and Fred and George are closer to each other than to him. Though he and Ginny are closer in age, they never hang out together.

The trio is often just a twosome, and those two are usually Hermione and Harry, and sometimes, it's just Harry alone. In *Sorcerer's Stone,* Ron's knocked out and Harry goes on alone; in *Chamber of Secrets,* Ron is trapped in the rockslide with Lockhart while Harry goes on alone to save Ginny. Over and over, it's the same old story, with Ron just outside the circle of the spotlight. In other instances, Hermione is the one left out, like when Harry and Ron take the Ford Anglia to school, or during most of *Chamber of Secrets*. And Harry is often left out, too. However, Ron feels this perhaps most acutely, with his family being so near, yet always just out of his reach. This loneliness bleeds into his relationships with Harry and Hermione. In *Deathly Hallows*, the Horcrux-Hermione voices Ron's deep loneliness when it says: "Least loved, always, by the mother who craved a daughter... Least loved, now, by the girl who prefers your friend... Second best, always, eternally overshadowed..." (375–76). But this loneliness is also exactly why Ron needs Harry and Hermione.

From Ron's loneliness we can learn the lesson of humility. He struggles through it, sometimes with jealousy, but in the end he's able to accept the occasional imbalances of friendship without letting them consume him. When, in the epilogue of *Deathly Hallows*, some of the kids are still staring at Harry, just as they did throughout the entirety of the series, Ron jokes that they're staring at him, not Harry: "It's me. I'm extremely famous" (759). With this last joke of Ron's, he acknowledges and accepts both the loneliness of his own, less-famous life, and of Harry's lonely fame, too. They will both continue to be lonely sometimes, and they will still continue to have each other.

And even Hermione experiences a kind of loneliness. She's a Muggle-born witch, which makes her an outsider. She has no siblings, and very few close friends outside the trio. And she's unafraid to show how brainy she is, which doesn't make you very popular as a teenager. But we can learn a kind of bravery from Hermione: Even though Hermione's identity means that she might sometimes be lonely, she doesn't once waver from who she is. Nothing stops her from being completely herself.

From the trio, we can see that loneliness doesn't go away, even amid a friendship like theirs. Even as late as the *Deathly Hallows*, when Ron and Hermione have sacrificed everything to go with Harry, Harry wakes in the middle of the night to see Hermione's "arm curved to the floor, her fingers inches from Ron's" (176). He suspects they might've been holding hands, and that old lonely ache opens again. But perhaps their friendship looks even lovelier after the loneliness they all endure, the way they always manage to come back together and know what the others need.

They are each other's surrogate family, a family of choice, the kind each had always wanted but hadn't quite found until they found each other. Like all families, they disagree, fight, hurt each other, and sometimes lose faith in each other and walk away, even when they know they should do better. But what makes the trio so special is that they aren't bound by family obligations. They always come back together because they want to. Hermione always throws her arms around one of the boys, Ron returns to the trio in the woods, and though Harry tries to do things alone, he always lets Hermione and Ron come along, and all three are stronger for it. A friend of mine likes to say that love is a choice, which sounds unromantic. But from the trio's friendship, we can see that the ultimate form of love and friendship is to say, over and over again: *I choose us.*

Not only do we need our friends, our families, or our surrogate families, but we need a broader community, too. Each time a character in the books is alone, everything becomes colder, more difficult. Sirius is depressed, alone at Grimmauld Place until the Order comes to the house for Christmas, and then

Sirius fills the house with decorations and singing and food—joy that his people are finally home *(Order of the Phoenix,* 479). And Harry feels an intense joy when Sirius finally signs his permission form to go to Hogsmeade in *Prisoner of Azkaban*—that permission slip is a kind of key into a community (433). For Harry, the permission slip says he's normal, that he's just another student with people at home who care about him. And that's why Ron's early friendship on the train is such a gift—he continually reassures Harry that he won't be the worst in his year, and helps Harry transition into the wizarding world as kindly and openly as he can. In the same way, even though Harry is technically safest at the Dursleys' house under the protection of his mother's sacrifice, he doesn't ever feel truly at home there the way he does at Hogwarts. Acceptance into a community is a kind of comfort.

But more than that, acceptance and friendship can be a real form of protection. When Hermione convinces Harry to start Dumbledore's Army in *Order of the Phoenix*, she creates the first real chance for unity in the series. The rest of the unity has been the temporary unity of high school—the unity of Gryffindor versus Ravenclaw, of Quidditch teams, of first years versus third years. It's in *Order of the Phoenix* that both Dumbledore and the Sorting Hat start to tell students that they should strive for real unity, and Hermione listens. But resistance to this idea is all around them, and has been for many years. Hagrid tells Hermione not to socialize too much with Viktor Krum because you can't trust foreigners (*Goblet of Fire,* 563); Harry doesn't want to start the D.A. because he doesn't trust that people outside the trio can believe him, or that they might want more than another famous story from him. It would have been easy for Harry to work with only Ron and Hermione, to make sure they stayed among themselves.

But Hermione insists on the D.A. And this broader community brings in Ginny, Neville, and Luna, who are all fighting their own kinds of loneliness. In *Half-Blood Prince*, Luna asks if the D.A. will be re-formed, now that Umbridge is gone, because "it was like having friends" (138). On the night that Dumbledore dies, and Hermione summons the D.A. after seeing the Dark Mark, Luna and Neville are the only ones who respond. "Harry knew why: They were the ones who had missed the D.A. most ... probably the ones who had checked their coins regularly in the hope that there would be another meeting" (642). And Ginny, the only girl in a family of brothers, is constantly being told what to do and who to date. But without this unexpected group, Harry, Ron, and Hermione would likely not have survived their journey to the Department of Mysteries in *Order of the Phoenix*. And the formation of Dumbledore's Army is what leads to the eventual defense of the castle in *Deathly Hallows*. Without Dumbledore's Army, the trio might never have reached beyond themselves, and would've been without the help of Ginny, Neville, and Luna, all three of whom save their lives more than once. At the battle at the Ministry in *Order of the Phoenix*, there's a scene where Neville carries Hermione, Luna carries Ginny, and Harry carries Ron (796). Without their friends to carry them, the trio would not have been able to escape. Their friends carry them even when it slows them down, even when it hurts.

Without community, we fail. Both Voldemort and Draco Malfoy don't have true friends, and both fail to do what they attempt. Of Voldemort, Dumbledore tells Harry: "Lord Voldemort has never had a friend, nor do I believe that he has ever wanted one" (*Half-Blood Prince,* 277). Malfoy refuses Snape's help in *Half-Blood Prince,* convinced Snape wants to steal some of his glory (324). After Ron abandons the trio in *Deathly Hallows,* Hermione—driven, focused, organized Hermione—is unable to make herself do the defensive magic they need to keep themselves safe (312). Without their friendships, they are weakened. And later, in the Battle of Hogwarts, when Harry goes off alone, he finds his head muddied without his friends: "Without Ron and Hermione to help him he could not seem to marshal his ideas" (612). When Ron is poised to destroy the locket Horcrux, sword in hand, he's frozen and unable to do so until he hears his friend Harry say his name (375). His and Harry's friendship allows them to destroy the Horcrux together. And it's Hermione saying Ron's name that allows him to find his way back to the trio again (384). Though in many ways Harry must undertake his final battle alone, it's his friends—Ron and Hermione with the basilisk fangs to destroy the Horcruxes, and Neville with the snake—who build a bridge strong enough for him to walk across. They all need each other.

And that's the point, isn't it? Our communities save our lives. Evil can drive communities apart or bring them together. When, in *Order of the Phoenix,* Dementors show up in Little Whinging and attack Harry and Dudley, Harry is forced to explain what's happening to his aunt and uncle. He says that the "arrival of the Dementors in Little Whinging seemed to have caused a breach in the great, invisible wall that divided the relentlessly non-magical world of Privet Drive and the World beyond" (37). In a time of danger, the walls dividing communities can come down. When Harry and Dudley are threatened by Dementors, Harry struggles to cast his Patronus. As Harry is about to be killed, the thought bursts into his head that he's never going to see Ron and Hermione again. And this, the thought of his friends, is what allows him to finally conjure a Patronus (18). His love for his friends is what saves him and allows him to save Dudley, bringing both the magical and Muggle communities together.

In *Harry Potter*, the community inhabitants protect each other from Dementors, Umbridge, and Voldemort. In our world and in theirs, too, communities try protect us from many kinds of hurt. They remind us that we are not alone. In *Half-Blood Prince*, Harry works up the courage to tell his friends about the prophecy, this thing that's singled him out yet again and made him feel alone once more. When he tells them that he believes either he or Voldemort must ultimately die at each other's hands, Ron and Hermione give him what he needs most: their presence. Hermione springs into action, looking for a book, and Ron immediately starts rooting for Harry. In that moment, Harry feels his tension loosen, just a bit. His friends are still with him, and their support beside him, "not shrinking from him as though he were contaminated or dangerous, was worth more than he could ever tell them" (99).

When we trust friends, we are saying that a small part of us belongs to them, and we keep a small part of them with us, too. We lose our friendships and we find them again. When Ron is disillusioned with Harry's quest for the Horcruxes and leaves to reunite with his family, Hermione stays. She stays even when Harry does not deserve it. And even Ron comes back, drawn toward them like a tightened seam. From Hermione, Harry, and Ron, we can learn the kind of humility and courage that friendship takes. Friendship means that you must be humble and vulnerable; you must sometimes think beyond yourself. This is why Voldemort never has true friends: Voldemort views this vulnerability as a kind of weakness. That vulnerability to make deep friendships takes courage—the courage to trust your friends and to *let* your friends support you, like Harry learns; the courage to ask for forgiveness, like Ron does; and the courage to grant that forgiveness, like Harry and Hermione do of Ron.

The friendships in Harry Potter are beautiful because they're imperfect. Harry can be cruel; Hermione is sometimes inflexible; Ron abandons them when things get difficult. Ron and Hermione must go away to the prefect carriage, Harry must sometimes do things alone, and Hagrid won't always be there for them. But they always choose to come back and learn to be better. They commit to their friendship again and again. They continue to meet at the Hogwarts Express, and even 19 years later, their children know to look for each other. Whether they are fighting for each other's lives or meeting each other to simply say hello at a train station, their friendship teaches us to keep showing up. They teach us that, when staring at a hill, we should stand next to our friends and tell each other that the climb doesn't look so bad. Thanks to the magic of friendship, that hill—or that troll in the bathroom—will always seem smaller.

PROTEGO: ON KINDNESS

When I was living in Boston, I took a yoga class every now and then. I wasn't a very flexible person and wasn't particularly good at yoga, but I liked the stretching and the low lights and the part at the end where we got to lay on our backs. One bad day, I went to class. I can't remember now what was upsetting me, only that I was living in a city where I hardly knew anyone, far from my family and my boyfriend, and I never asked for help or told anyone when I was miserable.

We were in downward dog pose, and I was hanging upside-down, staring at my toes and being cruel to myself about the fact that I wasn't more flexible, when the yoga teacher came past. I pushed on my hands, trying to do an A+ downward dog. I wanted to win the yoga class. The teacher put a hand on my lower spine and made a small hip adjustment, and the stretch burned again down the backs of my legs. She then crouched down for a moment so she was closer to my ears and whispered, "It'll be okay."

I can't remember what upset me or that yoga teacher's name, but I remember her small, intuitive, empathetic kindness on that day, and I've carried that hot coal with me for many years since. She, someone who barely knew me, had been able to understand what I needed in that moment, and gave me that kindness. Like the spell *Protego*, kindness like that can serve as a shield—it fends off the harm of the world for just a moment. For many, myself included, kindness does not come naturally. I used to tell people that I wanted to be remembered most for being nice. But nice is not the same as kind. While being nice is more about trying to appear a certain way, kindness requires an awareness of others that being nice doesn't.

For some, like Hagrid, that kind of empathy and the kindness that results don't require any work at all. They're reflexive. Aside from Mrs. Weasley's cooking, Hagrid's love and care for all creatures, no matter how ugly or terrifying, is the best example of kindness in the series. Hagrid has every reason to be cynical and selfish, after his mother leaving him when he was very young and after his father's death. But instead, Hagrid's completely unafraid to give all he has to his animals. He risks burning his house down to raise baby Norbert, the dragon, and keeps Buckbeak the hippogriff in his house when Buckbeak's been scheduled for execution because, well, it's Christmas and he can't just leave him outside. His kindness for the animals is what keeps the students of Hogwarts (mostly) safe from the creatures in the Forbidden Forest. Hagrid's kindness toward animals that could harm humans allows for a peace between them that might not exist otherwise.

Even more difficult, perhaps, than trying to take a Blast-Ended Skrewt for a walk is being kind to people who don't appreciate or deserve it. Arthur Weasley never fails to show kindness to the Dursleys, no matter how much they openly hate him. In *Goblet of Fire*, some of the Weasleys explode through the Dursleys' fireplace to take Harry to the Quidditch World Cup. The Dursleys, in their shock and horror, are unable to say a word. Arthur, though, won't give up. He makes sure to ask, "Having a good holiday, Dudley?" (47). Later, Dumbledore, too, insists on sitting with the Dursleys and trying to have a drink with them, even as they refuse, their glasses smashing them on the head. Some might read this as a kind of insistence on politeness, but to me, it's an insistence on kindness. The Dursleys certainly haven't shown kindness to Arthur Weasley or to Dumbledore, and most of us would understand if they left with Harry without saying a word to the Dursleys. But the point is that they do not. Arthur and Dumbledore can teach us to be kind when it doesn't make us feel good at all—to insist, through our own kindness, that even unpleasant people are worthy of our kindness.

Until they aren't, of course. At the end of that same chapter, Arthur and Harry start to leave and when Harry says goodbye, the Dursleys don't answer. Arthur then says, "You aren't going to see your nephew till next summer.... Surely you're going to say good-bye?" (48). The Dursleys grudgingly do. But Arthur Weasley is a beautiful example of the way we must be kind, especially when it's not easy, and also how our kindness should have limits. Arthur stops being as kind and solicitous to the Dursleys to try and enforce their kindness toward Harry. His directness in phrase is in service of someone else. Even his command to the Dursleys is still kind—though the recipient of that kindness is now no longer the Dursleys, but Harry. (Although perhaps teaching the Dursleys some kindness could be seen as an additional kindness of Arthur's.) Many, especially women, are taught the garbage rule that we must be nice and kind to everyone always. Arthur Weasley and Dumbledore would conditionally agree; be kind until you do not need to any longer.

Hermione presents an even more radical version of kindness— being kind to her enemies. When Barty Crouch Jr. (posing as Professor Moody) turns Malfoy into a ferret in *Goblet of Fire* and bounces him around, Hermione is the only one worried that Malfoy could actually be hurt. When the trio, along with Luna, Neville, and Ginny, are fighting for their lives against Death Eaters in the Department of Mysteries in *Order of the Phoenix*, and one of the Death Eaters ends up with his head turned into an infant head, Hermione refuses to let Harry curse him. As justification, she says, "You can't hurt a baby!" (791). She's the sole person in the series who seems to care at all about the slavery of house-elves. Even when her life is being threatened, Hermione can see a kind of innocence in others. For her, Malfoy, the Death Eater, and house-elves are all victims of circumstances beyond their control, and so they deserve to be spared, even if it's in the smallest of ways. By contrast, it's not until *Deathly Hallows* that Harry realizes he should be kind to Kreacher, the house elf he inherited from Sirius's family, and that Ron realizes that the way to Hermione's heart is to be kind to her.

I don't know if I can reach Hermione's level of kindness. I'm not even sure it's advisable. But I admire Hermione for her commitment to her own moral code of not harming others. I could write about Hermione's kindness for pages—she has a great sense of emotional intelligence, and often knows when others need from her without their having to ask. In *Deathly Hallows*, after Harry discovers Dumbledore's involvement with the dark wizard Grindelwald, Hermione seems to know what Harry has lost, and that he doesn't want to talk about it. She leaves him alone outside their tent, but pauses for a moment to touch him gently on the head. Her kindness is a form of bravery—she's kind even when there's no benefit to her. She is unselfish with her kindness. She is unfailing. Her kindness is a quiet democratic force, like rain—all things around her will be touched.

As the young characters grow up, their kindness evolves. One type of kindness that's only become obvious as I've reread the books as an adult is the kindness of young people as they take care of adults. Though Hagrid is, in many ways, a kind of parental figure to Harry, the trio ends up taking care of him more often than not. In *Prisoner of Azkaban*, after Malfoy gets slashed by Buckbeak in Hagrid's first Care of Magical Creatures lesson, the trio finds Hagrid drinking in his hut. Seeing his distress, Hermione grabs his tankard, insists he's had enough to drink, and pours it out, keeping him from likely worse harm. Later, when they get the news that Buckbeak will be executed, both Ron and Hermione offer to make a cup of tea. Ron says, "...it's what my mum does whenever someone's upset" (219). Hagrid teaches us a lesson, if an unintentional one—he teaches us how those who've always cared for us, our parents and protectors, those who seem infallible, might need care, whether we're ready to give it or not. He teaches us how growing up will equalize us all, and will require selfless kindness.

The opportunities for young people to care for adults multiply as the books get more and more serious, and as the generational divide between the young people and the adults begins to disappear. This kindness requires a role reversal and feels a bit embarrassing to all involved. After the Quidditch World Cup, when Mrs. Weasley is upset about the Death Eaters' appearance, Hermione makes *her* a cup of tea. In *Order of the Phoenix*, Harry becomes very concerned about Sirius and doesn't want to leave him alone, lonely at Grimmauld Place (though he'd *never* say so to Sirius's face). And perhaps worst of all is when Harry feeds Dumbledore the potion in the cave while they retrieve the locket Horcrux. In that cave, Harry must comfort Dumbledore many times, even as he forces Dumbledore to drink the terrible potion. Even after they leave the cave, Harry continues to physically support Dumbledore and worry about his health. At this moment, Harry is like a child caring for his elderly parent. There is both love and cruelty in the type of kindness Harry shows, the type of kindness for others means making them do something that they hate, but that needs to be done.

The tragedy of this incredibly kind interaction is that, although it's painful for both of them, Harry doesn't realize these are his last moments with Dumbledore. Here, their roles have reversed, and Harry is the one reassuring Dumbledore that it will be okay. Even though Harry's kindness doesn't feel like a kindness, the moment is a gift to both of them.

On the way to my aunt's funeral, I held her wife's hand in the back of the limo. I resented it. I hated having to be the adult when I was grieving, too. It's not an easy task to do what the trio does in the books, and begin to take care of the adults as the adults have taken care of them. We want to resist this growth. But when children take care of the adults, it is the ultimate kindness of repaying the kindness that has been given to us.

When I started this chapter on kindness, I wanted to write you a story about small kindnesses in my life, as there have doubtless been many. But I sat and couldn't think of a single one. I wrote this chapter one painful sentence at a time. Kindness like Hermione's, Hagrid's, and Harry's sometimes feel rare, and as difficult to find as it is to describe. But that's not right. Look again, and that kindness can surround us like water—that cab driver who helps you with your crutches, the friend who says they believe in you when you need to hear it, your mother being so glad to hear about what you ate for lunch today. We can create kindness with a cup of tea or an "everything will be fine" when someone needs it. We can be the person to whom someone might say, as Dumbledore does to Harry in *Half-Blood Prince*, "I am not worried, Harry... I am with you" (578).

FLAGRATE: ON PREJUDICE AND RESPECT

ϟ ϟ ϟ

In 2004, I started saying "my aunt and her wife." My Aunt Pam married a woman named M, and they had a daughter together. I've known my whole life that my Aunt Pam was gay, though the people around me couldn't quite bring themselves to use that word. They weren't sure what words to use. Aunt Pam had a lot of "friends"; Aunt Pam lived with women. As a kid, I accepted it blindly, the way kids do—it made sense that, when you loved someone a lot, you lived with them so that you could be near them every day. That made much more sense to me than any vegetable, or why my hair always looked so dumb. Although kids sometimes see things in absolutes, kids are also more willing to accept the world and people for what they are. Until, of course, they are taught otherwise. Like *Flagrate*, the spell Hermione uses to mark a door with a red X, prejudice marks some people as *other*, a fiery X in our minds.

When my aunts first married in 2004, they lived in Massachusetts because gay marriage wasn't yet legal everywhere. They wanted to be somewhere where M could legally adopt their daughter (to whom Aunt Pam had given birth) in case anything ever happened to one of them. They had to choose where they'd live, from few options, a place where they'd have the right that heterosexual parents never question when they give birth: their right to a relationship with their child. Here I think of Dumbledore's sister Ariana, and how she suppressed her own magic after she'd been attacked by Muggle boys, and had to be kept away from other witches and wizards. Or of the giants, forced to live in the mountains after being targeted and hunted. Prejudice forces some to live a kind of half-life, a separate life, an *other* life. But like we learned from *Brown vs. Board of Education*, separate is not equal.

M died suddenly of ovarian cancer in 2014. Thanks to the country's long-overdue support of their marriage, my Aunt Pam and their daughter, my cousin, have access to her estate (something they wouldn't have had she died even a few years earlier), and they will be able to live comfortably. The point is that, when I tell people what happened to my family, I don't even have the right language to do it. I can say, "My aunt's wife," but that doesn't sound right. She was my aunt's wife, yes, but she was more than just her marital status to someone I'm related to. She was as equally my aunt as my blood-related Aunt Pam. But when I tell people my aunt died, they inevitably ask, "How's your uncle doing?"

My dear friend Lindsey married her long-time girlfriend Greta in January of 2017, 14 years after my aunts were married and two years after gay marriage was legalized in the United

States. They were ready to be married, but they also felt afraid that their rights might be taken away. The day was cold, a Boston winter, but Lindsey wore a dress anyway, and we all walked out into the snowy Harvard Arboretum to watch them get married. No one cared that our tears froze. Afterward, we drank champagne and danced to Michael Jackson. Lindsey's family posted on social media about a wedding. They posted pictures of the dusting of snow and of the homemade cake. But they couldn't quite bring themselves to post pictures of the two brides together. We like to think we have come far, that we're moving away from prejudice, but the tide is slow to come in, and it seems we'll have to continue beckoning it again and again.

Even in the world of *Harry Potter*, where enough magic exists to make people fall in (temporary) love, to be lucky, to make things appear and disappear and transform, their magic still isn't quite enough to move beyond prejudice. Prejudice appears in many forms over the course of the series—racial prejudice, magic/nonmagic prejudice, xenophobia, class prejudice, and sexism. No non-human creature is permitted to use or carry a wand. In *Harry Potter*, the power of wandlore is literally only allowed for one race. Of course, other races have their own kind of magic—the goblins with their metalwork, the house-elves with their magic, the centaurs with their divination. But the wizarding race has assumed the wand is the most powerful magic, and thus they have taken it all for themselves, to assume control, and out of fear of it being turned against them. It's exemplified with the portrait of Sirius Black's mother, which, when disturbed, screams things like "half-breeds, mutants, freaks... abomination, shame of my flesh" (*Order of the Phoenix,* 78) at people. She's the voice of a continuing legacy of wizarding nobility's prejudice against pretty much anyone who isn't exactly like the "pure"-blooded, wealthy, Muggle-hating Black family. And her language—*abomination*—is familiar to our own culture. In it, we hear the reverberating echoes of accusations against LBGTQ people and others.

Prejudice takes many forms in the *Harry Potter* series, but the most frequent is racism—not only among magical races like the wizarding race, goblins, giants, and house-elves, but also between the wizarding race and Muggles. Though most witches and wizards adopt a kind of live-and-let-live mentality, Muggles are still widely regarded as stupid and flawed for not having magical abilities. We only need to look at the way the wizarding community treats Arthur Weasley for his interest in Muggles to understand the prejudice against them. Arthur himself talks about Muggle-baiting (bewitching Muggle objects to harass or hurt Muggles), which most witches and wizards consider a harmless joke, as "an expression of something much deeper and nastier" (*Order of the Phoenix,* 153). When Death Eaters attack at the Quidditch World Cup, Hermione is the first and only magical person to worry about the nearby Muggles' safety. And even though Squibs are born to magical families, because they can't properly do magic, they're outcasts and treated as if they're Muggles—as if they're inferior.

It's no surprise, then, that "Mudblood" is considered one of the worst things you can call a person—highlighting their "dirty" blood, their relationship to someone non-magic. When Lily Potter, Harry's mother, asks young Severus Snape whether being Muggle-born will affect her, Snape pauses for just a moment, and then says, "No...it doesn't make any difference"

(*Deathly Hallows,* 666). We could read this as an attempt to stop the cycle of prejudice; but instead, we understand that Snape is lying to Lily. Because he loves her, he doesn't want to tell her the painful truth—that yes, indeed, her Muggle blood does matter very much. And when Lily is upset with her Muggle sister, Petunia, Snape tries to reassure her by saying that Petunia is "only a—" and then stops himself. But we understand what he's stopped himself from saying: Muggle. Only a Muggle. She is less than us, Snape wants to say.

And Petunia is equally guilty of her own prejudice. After Lily is headed for Hogwarts, Petunia scoffs that Lily is headed for "a special school for freaks. You and that Snape boy...weirdos...It's good you're being separated from normal people. It's for our own safety" (669). Petunia is justifying her own cruelty, as if Lily deserves it. Prejudice like Snape's, Petunia's, and later, Voldemort's, sustains itself because those who are prejudiced believe those on the other side have earned it.

The most extreme example of prejudice in the series is, of course, Voldemort's. We know Voldemort's type—power-hungry, orphaned, abandoned, selfish, and self-hating. Half-Muggle himself, Voldemort turns his self-hatred outward, like tyrants throughout our real-life history always do, and punishes others to account for the punishment he feels he deserves himself. Rather than betray a perceived weakness within himself, he enacts violence upon others to protect himself from confronting his own demons. There is no room for self-reflection or nuance to escape from Voldemort's hatred and violence—in his own words, speaking through Quirrell as early as *Sorcerer's Stone*, he says, "There is no good and evil, there is only power, and those too weak to seek it" (291).

Perhaps the second most obvious source of prejudice in the series is our favorite witch to hate: Dolores Umbridge. Umbridge's form of oppression is her devotion to a system that clearly favors some over others, and creates a hierarchy of wizards and witches (and Umbridge herself) above all else. If the status quo keeps people like Umbridge in power, then Umbridge will protect the status quo at all costs. Over the course of *Order of the Phoenix*, Umbridge manipulates Hagrid into his poor teaching evaluation by ensuring he fits into stereotypes about stupid, slow giants; she's in favor of having merpeople rounded up and tagged, and refers to Lupin, Hagrid, and the centaurs as "half-breeds." Of the centaurs, she quotes to their faces a law that describes centaurs as having "near-human intelligence" (754). In Umbridge's world, magical humans are at the top of the hierarchy, and everyone else is subhuman, lesser.

Prejudice like Voldemort's and Umbridge's arises from their own fears they'd never admit to having. They are both so afraid to lose their own perceived sense of power and superiority that they make sure those who oppose them are worth hating. Oppressors like Voldemort and Umbridge invent their own stories to justify their perception. They want to be in power, so those they see as beneath them must have done something to deserve it. This mindset is obvious among those who follow people like Voldemort: In *Deathly Hallows*, his Death Eaters have taken over Hogwarts after Dumbledore's death. Alecto is teaching students that Muggles are "like animals, stupid and dirty" (574), and that they drove witches and wizards into hiding by being vicious. Thus, killing Muggles or Muggle-borns is justified. According to them, as Voldemort comes back to power, "the natural order is being reestablished" (574). This sounds an awful lot like the false justification for slavery in the United States: The oppressors create a false enemy in order to put themselves back in power again. Rather than face their own fears, they create fear among others. To those who want power for power's sake, fear and respect feel like the same thing.

But again, we expect racism and prejudice from people like Petunia, Voldemort, and Umbridge, people who feel threatened or afraid. Voldemort's hatred of Muggles and insistence on pureblooded wizard lines isn't the kind of hatred we can learn from. Even children reading the *Harry Potter* series know that Voldemort and Umbridge are supposed to be the bad guys. The more insidious kinds of prejudice are those that creep downward from places of power and infect on a smaller, day-to-day level, a grain of sand in our eye that multiplies, nearly invisible, but scratches us open nonetheless. In *Order of the Phoenix*, Sirius explains to Harry the kind of slow prejudice that led to Voldemort's rise: "...there were quite a few people, before Voldemort showed his true colors, who thought he had the right idea about things... They got cold feet when they saw what he was prepared to do to get power, though" (112). On a small scale, this kind of prejudice is easy to discount. It's easy to talk yourself out of the small injustices we see or create. How frequently do we hear the justification that stereotypes come from somewhere? Or that it's just a joke, and we should calm down? Voldemort's prejudice is an extreme, but everyday instances of prejudice are far more common and are what allow ideas like Voldemort's to take hold. It's this type of prejudice that we must reject in our day-to-day lives. Prejudice and oppression do not begin with an *Avada Kedavra* or an atomic bomb; they move slowly, like the slow rise of floodwaters, eating away at earth until the ground collapses beneath us all before we know to move.

Perhaps the hardest prejudice in the series to face comes from someplace less obvious: Ron Weasley. Ron is not evil, of course, but complex in the way we all are, caught in a crosswind of assumptions and fears. Ron himself often faces class prejudice, as he's repeatedly teased and mocked for the Weasleys' perceived poverty. But he also displays some of the wizarding community's prejudices that have been built into their everyday lives, running beneath the surface of wizard and witches' interactions like a magnetic field. In *Prisoner of Azkaban*, the trio is confronted with the fact that their Professor Lupin is a werewolf. Hermione has figured it out (of course), but she has kept the secret—she knows that Lupin faces being fired, and perhaps worse, if his secret is discovered. But when it appears that Lupin has turned against the trio to support Sirius Black (before Sirius's innocence is revealed), Ron reveals his own bias. When Ron cries out in pain from his broken leg, Lupin moves toward him with concern, and Ron says, "Get away from me, werewolf!" (345). In his moment of fear, Ron stops even recognizing Lupin by his name and instead calls him by his race.

Ron demonstrates this same kind of prejudice later, in *Goblet of Fire*. As the trio learns about Hagrid's giant heritage, Ron fills in a clueless Harry on some giant characteristics: "They just like killing, everyone knows that" (430). Hermione thinks this prejudice against giants is a kind of bigotry, but Ron disagrees—he just shakes his head in disbelief (434).

While we might be tempted to write Ron's ideas off as a part of his youth, or as a part of the culture he grew up with, and to think he might grow out of them, that would be a mistake. We see how the ideas of a 14-year-old are enlarged and distorted in the broader culture, and how that creates real harm in Hagrid and Madame Maxime's lives. Later in the book, Madame Maxime is accused of attacking Barty Crouch because she's part giant. After Hagrid's giant background is exposed, he receives letters that say "you're a monster and you should be put down" (544), as if he is an animal. The ideas in the letters are only a few, nastier steps ahead of Ron's ideas. These ideas continue to catch: Later, this prejudice against giants is what makes them turn to Voldemort. What have wizards and witches ever done for them, but hurt and demonize them? Why would they join with their oppressors? Those small words ("they just like killing") build, a snowflake to an avalanche.

Ron's ideas *are* part of his youth and are certainly part of what he's been taught. But without confronting those ideas, they continue to spread. Ron is capable of evolving (when we see him, in the last pages of the series, finally worrying about house-elves instead of telling Hermione to shut up about it), but it takes work. We must do as Hermione does when we see prejudice like Ron's in our own lives: We must not ignore it or assume it'll go away. Like Dumbledore says, "Indifference and neglect often do much more damage than outright dislike" (*Order of the Phoenix,* 834). We owe it to the future to be the person who speaks up—even when it's difficult or awkward, like it was for Hermione to speak on house-elves—rather than the person who stays silent and lets the damage continue.

And speaking of Hermione and the house-elves: It's finally time to address them. Perhaps the most difficult thing about rereading the *Harry Potter* novels as I've gotten older is facing the way the house-elves are treated. In *Goblet of Fire*, as they watch the way Barty Crouch treats his house-elf, Winky, Sirius tells Ron that, "If you want to know what a man's like, take a good look at how he treats his inferiors, not his equals" (525). But how are the house-elves treated by wizards other than Crouch? With the exception of Dobby, the house-elves are essentially slaves (including Kreacher, Sirius's own house-elf). They work for no pay. They seem to have always worked for no pay. They must punish themselves if they disobey their masters, who they literally call "master." Much of Hogwarts's magic (the gorgeous dormitories, the insanely indulgent feasts) isn't the result of Dumbledore's power, but instead comes from the unpaid, invisible work of the house-elves. Even at Hogwarts, the refuge for lost boys and girls and misfits, almost none of the students realize (or care) about the house-elves in the castle with them.

We discover later that the house-elves have magic that the wizards do not. The house-elves at Hogwarts do not seem bound by the same level of cruel magic as Dobby or Winky were under their former masters. They say that they enjoy what they do and don't mind the lack of pay (with Dobby again as the exception). But does it matter? Out in the world, the house-elves are not seen as equals to witches or wizards. Voldemort uses Kreacher the house-elf to test for poison. But so does the arguably more benign Slughorn (and Harry, when he discovers this, hides it from the equality-minded Hermione). Even Sirius is guilty of the very prejudice he warns Ron against. Dumbledore tells Harry that he does not think

Sirius "ever saw Kreacher as a being with feelings as acute as a human's...Kreacher is what he has been made by wizards" (*Order of the Phoenix*, 832).

Nearly Headless Nick, the Gryffindor ghost who's lived in the castle for nearly 500 years, believes that house-elves are at their best when they're invisible: "That's the mark of a good house-elf, isn't it, that you don't know it's there" (*Goblet of Fire*, 182). House-elves are most acceptable to wizards when it appears they don't exist at all. This might remind the reader of when the Dursleys force Harry to stay in his room, pretending he doesn't exist. But the same outrage we feel for Harry doesn't seem to extend to the house-elves, for whom not existing is supposed to be a good thing. The prejudice is old and far-reaching. What kind of life would free house-elves have? Though they say they're happy, what choice do they have? There is no such thing as happiness if slavery is your only option in life.

And then there's Dobby. Dobby must feel an affinity for Harry not only because he's The Boy Who Lived and needs to be protected, but also because they've both come from homes where they're trapped and mistreated. And we must give credit to Harry for recognizing the interaction between Lucius Malfoy and Dobby as a dysfunctional, abusive one, and realizing that Dobby needs to be freed. Since Dobby can't free himself, Harry uses his power to free him. This is a lesson we can learn: If we have power, we need to use it to work for those who don't.

But what does Dobby do with his freedom? He ends up at Hogwarts, doing the same work he would've done before.

Granted, he's paid this time, and treated better. But when he and Hermione try to rally the other house-elves and wizards to campaign for more equality like Dobby's, they're shunned at every turn (even by Ron and Harry). Though Dobby's freedom is of course important, it's hard to feel like Dobby's freedom has a broader impact when the system doesn't change around him.

Dobby's impact is that in the end, Dobby is the hero of Harry's story, not Harry. When the trio is trapped in Malfoy Manor where Hermione is being tortured and Voldemort is on his way to kill them all, it's Dobby's magic that allows him to Apparate away. Without Dobby, they would all be dead. But it's Dobby who takes the knife to the chest, not anyone else. It's Dobby's grave that Harry must dig. And Dobby continues to save Harry, even after death—while digging Dobby's grave, Harry discovers the clarity he's been looking for: He chooses destroying the Horcruxes over uniting the Deathly Hallows and gains the conviction to decide what to do next, setting the plot of the end of the series in motion. Though Dobby is free, he still ultimately gives his life for wizards, which is what house-elves have been doing all along.

The house-elves in the books retain a kind of power: They have the ability to turn the plot of the story, like a hand on a rudder, if only the wizards would think to ask them. The house-elves are the keepers of knowledge and secrets that the wizarding community can't imagine or understand. It's Winky who holds the secret that Barty Crouch Jr. is alive and rallying for Voldemort. It's Dobby who knows that the Chamber of Secrets has been opened, who knows the Malfoys trade in Dark Magic, who knows how to open the Room of

Requirement. And it's Kreacher who knows about the locket Horcrux. But Winky is ordered to shut up, Dobby must punish himself, and Sirius Black's neglect of Kreacher leads to his own death. Voldemort and Sirius both underestimate house-elves, and both are hurt because of it.

As Hermione says, "I've said all along that wizards would pay for how they treat house-elves. Well, Voldemort did...and so did Sirius" (*Deathly Hallows,* 198). And so, too, does Harry—though he's not as prejudiced as some of the others around him, he pays in grief for Dobby's sacrifice (and for Sirius's death). Prejudice doesn't only affect those toward whom it is directed—the harm of prejudice is as contagious as a disease.

Where do we go from here? The situation of the house-elves in the books is troubling. It doesn't seem to speak to freedom. In the last sentence of the book before the epilogue, Harry doesn't wonder if Kreacher is okay, or think about freeing Kreacher—he wonders if Kreacher might bring him a *sandwich*. What have we learned about prejudice? We have *not* learned that everything is okay, resolved, or that we should all just get along with each other. We've learned that there's still a lot of work to do.

One of the teachers for this lesson is, of course, Dumbledore. In *Half-Blood Prince*, Dumbledore leans against the wall of the Astronomy Tower, about to die. Malfoy, in explaining his plan, wand pointed at Dumbledore's chest, insults Hermione by using the word "Mudblood." The following conversation then occurs:

"'Please do not use that offensive word in front of me,' said Dumbledore.

Malfoy gave a harsh laugh. 'You care about me saying "Mudblood" when I'm about to kill you?'

'Yes, I do,' said Dumbledore, and Harry saw his feet slide a little on the floor as he struggled to remain upright" (589).

And even rude, brash Snape, in the moments before he secretly drops the sword of Gryffindor in the Forest of Dean for Harry to discover in *Deathly Hallows*, can teach us this lesson. When the portrait of Phineas Nigellus tells Snape where the trio is camping, he, too, calls Hermione a Mudblood. Even when no one is watching, when avoiding prejudice isn't a kind of performance, Snape still says, "Do not use that word!" (689). In the face of prejudice, the easy and cowardly thing to do is to ignore it, which Snape has done before. But here, he does the hard thing and says something.

Even in his last moments of life, Dumbledore is committed to respecting others. Even in secret, with a portrait who's not even a real person, Snape is committed to respect. We should learn to do the same, because showing respect for each other and rejecting prejudice is not a matter of politeness. It requires constant defense and strength. If prejudice starts on a small scale, then rejecting prejudice does, too. We must refuse to be quiet. We must, like Hermione, be unafraid to work for those who are facing prejudice. We should post the picture of the two brides and tell them we are so happy for them. We should be unafraid to say "Do not use that word." We should be brave enough to say, when asked if we care, "Yes, I do."

SONORUS: ON THE POWER OF WORDS

When I was applying to colleges, I asked my high school English teacher for a letter of recommendation. I'd been in multiple classes of his and had been his TA in my senior year. I'd taken a bunch of English AP tests. I filled notebooks with observations. I spent lunch times with other nerds in his classroom. English was my *thing*.

My teacher gave me his letters in sealed envelopes, according to the directions, with his signature across the seal of each. I used one for one school, but I changed my mind about the other school and decided not to apply. That meant that I had an extra letter. I knew I shouldn't read it, but who could resist? I was certain it was full of effusive praise for me.

And I'm sure it *was* full of praise, as this English teacher was a kind man and understood the point of recommendation letters. But I don't remember any of it. The thing I remember about that letter was a single sentence: "Jill's not a good writer, but she tries hard."

It's been 12 years since then, but that sentence has never left me. I'm sure this English teacher would be horrified if he knew how that sentence follows me like a shadow. Though it was certainly unintentional, the simple fact of it—*Jill is not a good writer*—had somehow illuminated the thing I was most afraid of. Those words, so cruel in their bluntness, suggest that even if I tried hard, the thing would remain true: I would never be what I wanted to be. Those words felt like my personal worst omen, a Grim foretelling an end.

⚡⚡⚡

Words are as important to the wizards and witches in *Harry Potter* as they are to Muggles. Like the spell *Sonorus*, which amplifies Fudge's voice at the Quidditch World Cup, words have the power to reach thousands. On a smaller level, too, words matter. We cheer whenever Harry uses *Expelliarmus* or when Hermione comes up with the right spell at just the right time. We learn that it matters whether you say that you "Levi-*o*-sa," not "Levio-*sa*." In the *Harry Potter* universe, it's also harder to deny that words can hurt us. Along with wands, words are a potent sense of power.

Harry grows up in an environment where words are the enemy. The Dursleys often punish him for saying the wrong thing. The word "Hogwarts" holds so much fear and power for the Dursleys that Harry's not even allowed to say it inside the house. They like Harry best when he's in his room, making no noise, and they can pretend he doesn't exist. His words are a sign of his existence, and the Dursleys feel the most power when Harry is silent. This is why we love when Harry gets sassy, like when Dudley tries to tease Harry in *Chamber of Secrets* over the lack of attention on his birthday, and brags that he knows what day it is. In response, Harry says, "Well done... So you've finally learned the days of the week" (9). Because Dudley is scared of Harry now that he's a wizard and he thinks Harry can hurt him back, Harry is able to regain a bit of his own power through his words for Dudley.

Silence can be a power of its own if it's chosen, but enforced silence, like the silence toward Harry, is abuse. It's not until *Deathly Hallows* that Harry refers to his own treatment as abuse. Harry finally uses the word after learning about Dumbledore's sister Ariana's isolation and wondering if her isolation meant that she was treated the same way he was: "Could Dumbledore have let such things happen? Had he been like Dudley, content to watch neglect and abuse as long as it did not affect him?" (177). Harry's own childhood silence has so shaped his life that he's even willing to question Dumbledore, the one whose words Harry has always trusted.

Voldemort proves he's just as afraid and ashamed as the Dursleys are, but for different reasons. Voldemort throws out the evidence of his father's name—Tom Riddle—and gives himself a new one. He's afraid that others will see him for exactly who he is: part-Muggle, part not-wizard, and worst of all, mortal. So he fashions himself a new name, one he "knew wizards everywhere would one day fear to speak" (*Chamber of Secrets,* 314). For him, his new name erases his own fear and shame and gives himself power—a new identity, one wholly his, and so twinned with violence that no one even wants to say it aloud. He wants even his name to be a form of violence.

But Voldemort forgets that words have their own power, beyond what we might do with them. Even as he attempted to get rid of his Muggle past, he doesn't quite succeed. He doesn't come up with a completely new name; rather, he reuses the letters of his old name. "Tom Marvolo Riddle" still haunts "I am Lord Voldemort." The old names hint at some alternate future he chose to destroy, some bit of humanity that still lived inside of him. He's not able to get rid of the power of his past completely. The name "Tom Riddle" holds more power than even Voldemort knew. And Dumbledore knows this—whenever he sees Voldemort, he insists on calling him Tom Riddle. For Dumbledore, this is a way of using words to reject Voldemort's power, and instead, point to the possibility of his humanity.

Voldemort believes that using his name creates fear, and in many, it does. But by creating that fear, Voldemort also accidentally created a space for bravery. Dumbledore agrees, and says in *Sorcerer's Stone* that we should "always use the proper name for things. Fear of a name increases fear of the thing itself" (298). Naming a thing can also help to lessen our fear; for example, when we find out the name for an illness we have, it's a form of comfort. When we name something, it moves from the realm of unknown to the known. Dumbledore teaches us to name the things that scare us, like Voldemort. Instead of using the names as an opportunity for fear, use them instead as a chance for bravery.

When Hermione finally uses Voldemort's name for the first time, it's to convince Harry to start Dumbledore's Army in *Order of the Phoenix*. She names Voldemort as a signal that she's serious, that she can be brave. Her goals are bigger than her fear. It's significant when Hermione starts to use Voldemort's name, especially because this moment is less about Voldemort than it is about Hermione. Using Voldemort's name lessens his power and gives some to her. She uses his true name in order to resist him.

Later, when Voldemort uses the Taboo in *Deathly Hallows* to find and punish those who use his name, that trace is the first thing that actually moves Harry forward in the path toward destroying the Horcruxes. Without being captured by the Snatchers and taken to Malfoy Manor, Harry would never have encountered Ollivander, who helps him, nor would he have found Dobby, who rescues him. It also allows him to disarm Malfoy, which means he ends up the true owner of the Elder Wand. Though saying Voldemort's name didn't dispel Harry or Hermione's fear, it inspired action and delivered them into their own bravest selves.

Perhaps this is partly why Harry is so unafraid of saying Voldemort's name, while most everyone else refuses to do so: For Harry, who was silenced because of the Dursleys' desire for power over and fear of Harry, he refuses to remain silent in the face of another evil. Of course, because he's been relatively isolated, it's easier for Harry to say Voldemort's name. He does not have the context for fear that other wizards and witches have. At the same time, because he's had to live in an environment of fear his whole life, saying Voldemort's name is a rejection of that fear. For Harry, saying "You-Know-Who" is like closing your eyes when something bad is coming. The bad thing is going to come—we might as well face it with our eyes open and our mouths loud.

And this is why, for Harry, more than anyone else, words are freedom. Becoming a wizard means learning words that give him literal power, and giving him a world where he can escape from the Dursleys. When Harry's wand is broken in *Deathly Hallows,* he grieves the loss for many days. For him, the loss of the wand is the loss of his magic words and the loss of his power, the most important part of who he is.

Words are bound up in the deepest and most secret parts of our identities. When Malfoy and others use hate speech ("Mudblood"), they are telling us about their own secret fears. Their words are a form of violence. "Words can never hurt us" is a lie. I'd love to tell you that my whole writing life was propelled by an old need to show someone that their words about me were wrong. I'd love to tell you that I didn't believe that professor for second, and that his words couldn't hurt me. But neither are quite true. Those words were power, though not in the way you might expect. Like in anyone's life, they were just a few of many that have built the skeleton of my own bravery and ambition. On their own, negative words are devastating. But they aren't everything. We can choose to live by some words and we can choose to defy others. In *Harry Potter*, we see that words are a catalyst for self-determination: With the words we choose, we say, yes, I am this, or no, I am not that. As much as our DNA, words make us. From *Harry Potter*, we learn again that words are power; words are magic.

IMPERIO: ON BREAKING THE RULES AND THE DANGER OF POWER

⚡⚡⚡

As a professor, I'm supposed to be in a position of power, but as an introvert, it's sometimes hard for me to step into the spotlight that being a professor requires. As a youngish, informal female professor, students and other professors often don't take me seriously. Within me is a constant pull between my personality, the power of the title, and the power that I don't always feel.

On the first day of each semester, I enjoy waiting outside a classroom and listening to students wonder what their professor will be like, without realizing their professor is standing right there beside them. I relish the joy and rush of satisfaction I feel when I walk to the front of the class and the students realize that I am their professor. I secretly love it when a student calls me "Professor," or when they come to me to ask forgiveness for something they've done wrong. But this rush frightens me. I don't want it to give me that much joy, to hold that kind of power over me. But the fact remains that it does.

Since I only rarely feel all-powerful in the classroom, or as a quiet writer and introvert in my everyday life, I seek that power in small ways. Once a week, I volunteer with Mounted Patrol as a part of the National Park Service, where I ride horses around the park's trails, hand out maps, and tell people about park rules. One day, after a week of heavy rain, the trail to the beach was marked closed due to a rockslide. I stood at the barrier for a moment, thinking about my lifelong boring desire to follow the rules (even now, as an adult, I worry about "getting in trouble" from vague authority figures). But not for long—I decided my baseball cap, with its National Park Service logo, made me qualified to cross the barrier. It didn't matter that the rules had probably been made to keep me safe. The rules did not apply to me. I wanted to go to the beach, so I stepped around the barrier and did it anyway. It was a stupid and small rule to break, but still, I felt great and powerful doing it.

The seductive dangers of power and questions about when to break the established rules surround the characters throughout the *Harry Potter* series. The novels offer us a roadmap of different paths we might take—when we might turn toward power and when we should turn away; when we should join forces, or when we should resist. Are we Percy, who gets too caught up in the rules? Or are we Barty Crouch, who, as we've seen, commits violence nearly equal to Voldemort's in the very fight against evil? Are we Dumbledore or Harry, who both struggle with power's temptation?

At face value, good rules and power structures are supposed to protect us. But the good (or harm) that rules impose depend on who's setting them. Just like prejudice, the kind of oppression that Voldemort wants does not start at the top. Oppression starts small, with rules: who sets the rules, who can own wands, who can be in charge, who can speak up, and who is forced to stay silent.

The biggest rule-follower in the series is perhaps not who you think it is (did you think Hermione?), but Percy Weasley. Percy serves as a kind of cautionary tale for what happens when we accept all rules and those who make them as an absolute power, without considering whether the rules are fair or just. Percy *loves* rules. He loves being near Barty Crouch and Cornelius Fudge, people who make and enforce the rules. To Percy (and to many of us), following the rules makes you a good person.

Percy sees following the rules as a kind of game he must play in order to have access to powerful people so he can then take some of that power for himself. Percy follows the rules, so he's Head Boy. Percy follows the rules, so he gets a job at the Ministry of Magic. Percy disapproves of Fred and George (and later Harry), who are definitely not rule-followers.

Percy's deference to rules and to powerful people who can help him get ahead has a surprising mirror: Draco Malfoy. Though Percy would hate to hear it, Malfoy has a similar mindset—he's always appealing to his father's position as a source of power. He even thinks that good O.W.L. scores are more about who you know than your skills (*Order of the Phoenix*, 707). But the paths the characters follow and how those paths twist can tell us something about power. Fred and George are seen as troublemakers, misfits, and goofballs with no respect for authority, while Percy is seen as the ultimate goody two-shoes suck-up. On the other hand, Malfoy, while not a rulebreaker, tries to get power and glory by aligning himself with those he sees as powerful. In the end, though, Malfoy fails to impress Voldemort and his family is cast out; Percy ends up alone, estranged from his family; and Fred and George are beloved. Percy eventually quits the Ministry, once it's exposed as corrupt, and must start over doing something else, while Fred and George end up as more traditionally successful, with their shop Weasleys' Wizard Wheezes raking in the Galleons. Percy's devotion to the power structure means that he eventually abandons the goodness of his family in order to get closer to power. From him, we can learn to step back and examine why we're following the rules, and who gets hurt when we do.

But it would be unfair to blame Percy. The desire for power is heady and addictive, especially if we feel we're doing the right thing. We all want to rise a little higher and be a little greater. Most of us would rather not be mediocre. It's not surprising, then, that Percy is an acolyte of Barty Crouch, another rule-follower. Barty Crouch's form of rule-following elevates him to a position of power, and from this position, he creates hierarchies of who is important (namely, those who help keep him in power) and who is not. Percy then absorbs this tendency to separate people into categories of who matters and who doesn't. When Crouch finds out Winky, his house-elf, disobeyed his orders to save her own life, he says, "I have no use for a house-elf who disobeys me.... I have no use for a servant who forgets what is due to her master and to her master's reputation" (*Goblet of Fire*, 138). Later, Percy parrots the same language: "A high-ranking official like Mr. Crouch deserves unswerving obedience from his servants" (154). Later, in *Order of the Phoenix*, Percy warns Ron to stay away from Harry—partially because he thinks associating with Harry means Ron might lose his prefect badge, and partially because he thinks it will help Ron improve his "prospects" after school (297). He also criticizes his father Arthur for not having enough ambition and implies that his father's behavior is why they're poor and not in a higher position (72).

In both Crouch and Percy, we can see echoes of the same sentiments upon which Voldemort builds his following: a sense of us versus them, the idea that their rules are good for all, and thus, that people who do not share their sense of the rules deserve to be crushed. From Percy and Crouch, we can learn to turn away from the toxic story that power sells us: that we are better than others, and that those others deserve what they get.

Perhaps the biggest near misses with power in the series are those of both Harry and Dumbledore. Dumbledore's magical talent means he's tempted by Grindelwald's grab for power, in the name of the "greater good." This is the greatest, most necessary, and most damaging self-deception of all tyrants and dictators: They believe they are doing the right thing. This deception leads Dumbledore toward creating hierarchies, just like Crouch and Voldemort do; assuming he is better and more worthy than others around him; and worst of all, leaving his family, who needs him. When he and Grindelwald fight over their difference of opinion, it's Dumbledore's sister Ariana who is accidentally killed. She pays the price for their power struggle, like the innocent always do. Dumbledore must grieve her death for the rest of his life, and must learn a hard lesson: He is "not to be trusted with power" (*Deathly Hallows*, 717).

Harry, on the other hand, rarely feels tempted by power until the very end. He's initially thrilled in *Goblet of Fire* when Cedric Diggory is the Hogwarts champion, which means Harry might be able to step *out* of the spotlight for once. He doesn't want to lead Dumbledore's Army, and he feels lost in *Deathly Hallows* as he tries to lead the trio on their quest for Horcruxes. But while Dumbledore is tempted by the kind of power that leads him away from his family, Harry is tempted by the Deathly Hallows, the kind of power that he believes will lead him *toward* his family. It's true that he thinks uniting the Deathly Hallows will allow him to beat Voldemort, but he's mostly tempted by the power of the Resurrection Stone, and the possibility of bringing his parents and Sirius back from the dead, even if it's only a shallow kind of half-life.

But in the end, Harry chooses to reject the power of the Deathly Hallows. He refuses the Elder Wand, even as Ron drools over it. When he has the choice, Harry chooses to do what will save others, rather than save only himself. Dumbledore tells us that "perhaps those who are best suited to power are those who have never sought it" (718). In our history as humans, we seem to need to learn this lesson the hard way, again and again, as we trample each other in our own desire for power.

And now, inevitably, we've built our way to discussing Voldemort and his quest for power. Dictators and tyrants like him know that we are afraid of change. Many want to ignore the problems that exist and keep things the way they've always been. Those people who want power will manipulate our fear and our desire to avoid upsetting the status quo in order to gain it. And that fear doesn't exist only in the oppressed—fear drives oppressors, too. As Dumbledore says in *Half-Blood Prince*, "Have you any idea how much tyrants fear the people they oppress? All of them realize that, one day, amongst their many victims, there is sure to be someone who rises against them and strikes back!" (510). Rereading this time around and seeing Dumbledore's death coming from a horrible mile away, I paid a lot of attention to young Tom Riddle—how he bullies others, how he's so sure that he's special and better than everyone else, how his fear of death and his self-hate make him grab for power and scream "TELL THE TRUTH" at people. Voldemort's words are terrifying because they are familiar. They echo the bullying language of dictators throughout history—language that demands its listeners step into a manufactured version of the truth, language that demands obedience. Twenty years after the books were first published, those words are terrifying because they *remain* familiar.

How do we respond to someone like Voldemort? Many of us might like to think we would run toward the metaphorical fire, but the truth is that, when the lives of others around us are threatened, we might want to withdraw and move inward. Some might take too much comfort in the rules, and allow corrupt and unfair rules to continue without questioning them, probably because those rules only affect others. It's easy to pretend nothing is wrong when the danger hasn't yet arrived at your door.

Over and over again, we see the adults in the series refusing to face the evil that's right in front of them. They refuse because facing the evil means challenge; it means change; it means uncertainty; it means upheaval. Lockhart shows up as the first person to avoid facing evil—when he gets the chance to actually face the Chamber of Secrets, a real danger better than all the exploits he lied about in his books, he tries to run. And then, of course, we have Peter Pettigrew, the ultimate symbol for refusing to resist corruption and evil. At the end of *Prisoner of Azkaban*, Sirius confronts Pettigrew about his betrayal of Lily and James Potter to Voldemort, which led to their deaths. Pettigrew pleads, "He was taking over everywhere! What was there to be gained by refusing him?" Sirius replies, "Only innocent lives, Peter!" (375). Pettigrew's fear and comfort in the way things are keep him from doing what's right. His fear is a brick tied to the ankles of all around him.

We see this fear on a broader scale, too, once Voldemort has returned but the wizarding community refuses to acknowledge it, accept it, or do anything about it. Our desire to keep things the same and to ignore difficulty is based in fear. Like the spell *Imperio*, which controls someone like a puppet, tyrants use fear to do the same. Sirius describes it like this: "...accepting that Voldemort is back would mean trouble like the Ministry hasn't had to cope with for nearly 14 years" (*Order of the Phoenix*, 94). Accepting Voldemort has returned means facing war and death. Since it's not yet affecting the Ministry directly, they prefer to just ignore it. The same goes for the citizens the Ministry governs: Lupin tells us that, "While the Ministry insists there is nothing to fear from Voldemort, it's hard to convince people he's back, especially as they really don't want to believe it in the first place" (94). When, in *Deathly Hallows*, Lupin tells the trio about the Muggle-born Registry being built and used as a kind of ethnic cleansing, Ron is in disbelief. He says, "People won't let this happen" (209). But Lupin corrects him: It is happening. The registry *does* happen. Similarly, Voldemort, like Hitler in Nazi Germany, makes rules that you must come forward with information, and if you don't, you must be punished as a traitor. For those whose families are threatened, the choice between outing your neighbors to save your family or keeping quiet to save others and risk your family is obvious. Many of us would choose our own families every time. When afraid, people will let things happen that they know they shouldn't. Tyrants like Voldemort depend on that fear. When confronted with rules or with an evil that disrupts business as usual, it's easier to do as children do: cover our faces and believe that we are invisible.

But, unfortunately, we cannot make ourselves invisible. We live in a world with others. Inaction keeps people like Voldemort in power longer. Had the wizarding community listened to Harry sooner, much of the bloodshed that came later could've been avoided. We should never have to arrive at the point of choosing between saving our family's lives under fear from threats, or saving the lives of others. But history keeps ending up there. The wizarding community knew what Voldemort was like—they'd experienced it before. They had foresight; the first wizarding war did not need to be repeated.

We must get better at reading the signs. We must get better at facing our own mistakes. But this is an extremely difficult lesson to learn. We seem to only be able to want to fight against tragedy after the tragedy has already occurred.

⚡⚡⚡

Just like oppression starts small, so, too, does resistance. The first form of resistance in the books comes, of course, from Hermione. In *Order of the Phoenix*, Umbridge has been installed as Defense Against the Dark Arts professor, where she begins class by immediately insisting that her students chant mundane phrases back to her, and asks them to read quietly from the textbook (239–240). Hermione then does something completely out of character: She disobeys. Instead of following Umbridge's directions, she sits silently with her hand in the air. Perhaps from her experience with Lockhart in *Chamber of Secrets*, Fudge in *Prisoner of Azkaban*, and Crouch-via-Moody in *Goblet of Fire*, Hermione has learned that authority isn't always to be trusted. Even as early as the sorting ceremony dinner that year, she sees right through Umbridge's attempt to keep Voldemort's return quiet, and her lack of legitimate authority. Hermione's hand in the air is a kind of silent protest.

Hermione's willingness to break the rules works like a rock splitting a river in two. Her choice to raise her hand and question Umbridge creates another option for her classmates. She makes it easier for others to follow behind her. After she questions Umbridge's course aims and Umbridge refuses to really answer her, her defiance gives Ron, Harry, Dean, and Parvati the bravery to put their hands in the air and question Umbridge, too. And later, when they form Dumbledore's Army, Hermione insists that they elect a leader democratically, rather than follow in Umbridge's footsteps and just appoint someone. From Hermione, we can learn to be leaders, to be the person who is willing to put themselves on the line to speak out against something unjust. Or we can be like Dean and Parvati, and look for chances to band together with a leader. We must look for opportunities to be brave and then take them.

Arthur Weasley, too, displays the courage of rejecting small-scale oppression. In *Deathly Hallows*, Harry masquerades as Runcorn, a wizard known for treating Muggle-born wizards harshly. Arthur, of course, doesn't realize that Runcorn is actually Harry, but it doesn't matter. Runcorn has faked the family tree of a wizard named Dirk Cresswell in order to falsely accuse a wizard of being Muggle-born, and Arthur confronts him. He says, "Dirk Cresswell is 10 times the wizard you are" (255). As a so-called pureblood wizard, Arthur Weasley knows that he's not likely to get in as much trouble under the prejudiced regime. This gives him a kind of resiliency and power that Muggle-born wizards don't have. Rather than taking this power and hiding away with his family, Arthur uses that power to stand up to Runcorn. Similarly, in *Deathly Hallows*, some witches and wizards cast protective spells over Muggle homes in their neighborhoods. And Harry refuses to work with Rufus Scrimgeour, the Minister of Magic after Fudge, because he's been unwilling to directly face Voldemort in the past. If we have power like Arthur or Harry or witches and wizards with wands, we have an even greater responsibility to be willing to stand up against oppression and violent power. Like the wizards protecting Muggles, we must be willing to be selfless with our power. We must protect and fight for others, especially when we ourselves are already protected—whether we are on a podium with a bullhorn or face-to-face with a bigot in an elevator.

One of the biggest lessons to learn about resisting the temptation of power and rejecting violent oppression is that we should work together. Voldemort works alone, and it wrecks him. Malfoy works alone, and he's disgraced. Whenever Harry or Dumbledore keep secrets and work alone, their power is diluted, and they make mistakes. Harry can defeat the evil of Voldemort not because he's an amazing wizard, but because he has an immense community behind him doing small acts that build to something larger. In the final scenes of *Deathly Hallows*, Voldemort brings Harry's presumably dead body to show off to his friends and his teachers to try to demoralize them. He uses silencing charms to try to keep the crowd quiet. But through their unified power, the charms don't hold. Even though Ron must be traumatized by seeing the dead body of his best friend, he manages to do what Hermione did before— reject authority. He yells, "He beat you!" (730) and the charm is broken for a moment so others can yell out, too. Voldemort, aware of the power of community, further tries to demoralize them by lying that Harry died running away to save himself. But they know the truth. Their small acts of bravery and resistance are what allow the tide to turn and Voldemort's evil to be defeated.

Versions of Voldemort will appear in our Muggle world again and again. Some of us might have the chance to accept different kinds of power, and we will have to decide what we should do with it; which paths we want to walk. The time will arrive when we have to "make a choice between what is right and what is easy" (*Goblet of Fire,* 724) and remember that "we are only as strong as we are united" (723). When we have the choice, we can learn from the *Harry Potter* novels not to be the person who hides away and hopes that things will improve. We must be the rocks that split the river. We must be willing to use our powers for good, and to protect each other. It will not be easy. And if we can't be the one person to stand up, like Hermione, then we must be the one who takes her outstretched hand and stands beside her.

RIDDIKULUS: ON LAUGHTER IN DARKNESS

In my high school senior year yearbook, next to my picture with too much hairspray and teeth freshly free from braces, I wrote a bio that included this: "I love to make people laugh, even if it's at me." At the time I thought that this would make me seem cool, but in an unassuming way, as in, "Hey, I'm so cool that I don't even care if you're making fun of me. That's how chill and cool I am." (I was definitely not that chill or cool.) My family always jokes that if I were on a sinking ship, I would make a joke before I ran for the lifeboats. Humor has always been a way for me to avoid facing what I probably should. But it's also a way for me to comfort those around me, and of controlling an uncontrollable situation. If I can make someone laugh, I've given them the smallest of breaks from whatever is hurting.

Even though I try to make other people laugh, I'm not that great at doing it for myself. As an introverted writer, I tend toward self-reflection and blue days that come and go like bad weather. It's impossible to laugh yourself out of your own sadness—you need help from someone else to get you out of your own head. One of my best sources of laughter is Alisa, one of my oldest friends. In seventh grade, I tried to point out some fuzz on my shirt and tell her that my sweater was shedding, but it came out as, "My shedder is sweating." Stupid, of course, but we laughed and laughed until we were crying, and we haven't stopped for 16 years. Every time we see each other, something will hit us just the same as it did back then—sometimes it's something truly funny, but often it's not. The trigger doesn't matter. What matters on my blue days is that I know the next time I'll see her there will be laughter, and that certainty keeps me moving forward to better days, every time. Lucky for me, too, I managed to marry someone who makes me laugh. I need that laughter like a shot of adrenaline.

When I tried to write this chapter, I was hoping it would be hilarious. I wanted to write you some Fred-and-George–caliber jokes. But the *Harry Potter* series is, for the most part, not funny. The books are full of darkness. But, like in our own lives, sometimes the best and funniest moments in the series happen when laughter seems the most impossible. Amid so much darkness, the books teach us that laughter will always come back again, no matter how much we feel like it won't. Like facing a boggart, the image of the thing we fear, and turning it into something that makes us laugh, laughter gives us a way to own the things that happen to us. We can shout *Riddikulus!* to banish our own hypothetical boggarts and make the things we fear become a little less fearsome.

The first few books are steeped in humor as we discover Harry's new world. Every new thing feels delightful and funny: Chocolate Frogs, Neville running back to his seat with the Sorting Hat still on his head, Hagrid's horrible cooking, Dumbledore's batty speeches, troll boogers, a flying car that goes rogue and does what it wants—the jokes go on and on. Those small laughs fade as the characters begin to grow up. Dumbledore's speeches become more serious. The innocence of the Sorting fades as the Sorting Hat calls for unity, and as Harry and the trio often miss the Sorting completely while they're off doing something else.

As the books progress away from their childhood lightheartedness, some of those moments of humor stay firmly present, no matter what else happens. The silliness of the ridiculous passwords to both Gryffindor tower and Dumbledore's office continues long after the trio is inclined to laugh at them. The characters are used to the passwords by *Chamber of Secrets*, but we, the readers, are not. (And our hearts break with Harry when, after Dumbledore's death, Harry goes to visit his empty office and there is no password, no laughter at all.) The silliness of the passwords is a reminder to us to look for the small moments of humor that the world gives us. Even if we've grown up and gotten used to her, the Fat Lady will still be posted at the entrance to Gryffindor tower, waiting to hear you say "*Mimbulus mimbletonia!*"

Even after the books have darkened, we can find humor in the mistakes the characters make with each other, which showcases our common humanity. After Harry and Cho kiss for the first time, Hermione sees Harry's face and asks if he's all right. Harry is silent, because "in truth, he didn't know whether he was all right or not" (*Order of the Phoenix*, 457). Amid Harry's fears about being somehow possessed by Voldemort, fears about Dumbledore ignoring him, and his dreams about the Department of Mysteries, we can laugh with Ron and Hermione about a confusing, too-wet kiss. And later in that book, when Harry has his vision of Sirius at the Ministry and is trying to rally people to help, he snaps at both Ginny and Luna in his anxiety and frustration. While Harry is certain Sirius is about to die, Luna gives us a moment to laugh by chiding him, "You're being rather rude, you know" (735). Even at Dumbledore's funeral, Grawp pats Hagrid on the back so hard that his chair sinks into the ground. At that moment, even Harry stifles the urge to laugh. These supporting characters remind us of the ways we can still laugh at ourselves. Even when our lives feel dire, we can try not to take ourselves quite so seriously. They give us permission to laugh at small mistakes and stumbles, even in the face of darkness.

Of course, the most obvious source of humor in the books is the Weasley twins. The Weasley twins are throwing snowballs at Voldemort (as Quirrell) as early as *Sorcerer's Stone* (194). While in the first few books Fred and George seem to exist only to crack the occasional joke, they become more and more important as the books progress. Their comic relief is necessary, like in Chapter 21 of *Goblet of Fire* when Hermione is trying to figure out how to get down into the kitchens to talk to the house-elves and the other Gryffindors are trying to figure out Harry's second clue for the Triwizard Tournament. Neville interrupts by turning into a canary (367). This is a small moment in the books—Fred and George use this as an opportunity to market their Canary Creams, part of what will become their Skiving Snackboxes, and the section ends right afterward. Hermione continues to disapprove of Fred and George using tricks to miss class. But this is the seed for all that will come later.

This moment leads to students using Skiving Snackboxes in droves, fainting and nosebleeding and puking in the very dark *Order of the Phoenix*, to resist Umbridge. Fred and George's fireworks display is their magnificent middle finger to Umbridge's and the Ministry's oppressive rules as they break free. Fred and George teach us that a sense of humor can be more than just a distraction. From their humor, we can learn to be fearless in our laughter, and that laughter can be as powerful as any magic wand when it comes to defeating darkness. Their sense of humor is a show of strength—they refuse to be beaten by oppression or by evil, and choose laughter and joy instead. By the last two books, in a Diagon Alley full of darkness—homeless witches and wizards, stores selling Dark Magic products, stores that were symbols of happiness and magic, like Ollivander's and Florean Fortescue's Ice Cream Parlor, boarded up and closed—their store, Weasleys' Wizard Wheezes, is the only bright spot. Their canary creams are like the proverbial canary in the coal mine, but instead of warning of danger, the canary comes out, as bright and reliable as the sun, reminding us that there's still happiness to come.

Fred and George's influence continually serves as a source of relief, an active kind of joy. In *Goblet of Fire*, amid the real fear that one of the Triwizard Champions might die (and the looming threat of the stirring Death Eaters), Dumbledore has the sense to hold the Yule Ball as a break. While Ron and Harry grump about girls or brood about Snape and giants, Fred and

Angelina are busy dancing so exuberantly that people stay away from them to avoid getting hurt (420). In *Half-Blood Prince*, Fred and George manage to intervene, even indirectly, during one of the book's most serious moments: Harry is telling Ron and Hermione about the contents of the prophecy, and that he believes he must either kill or be killed. Hermione is holding a small telescope, which then punches her in the face (98). Even as Harry is recognizing his own mortality, Fred and George's inventions refuse to stay despondent and give the trio a much-needed break. Instead of thinking of humor as a kind of avoidance, we can learn from Fred and George that their relentless efforts to laugh are a form of strength and selflessness—their humor is not only for themselves, but a way to bolster those around them. Their humor refuses to be beaten down, and the world around them needs it.

Fred and George aren't jesters. Their humor isn't self-conscious or arrogant. They take their humor very seriously. They understand that the need for their humor is so great, so important, that they're willing to leave their education behind to open Weasleys' Wizard Wheezes. Nowhere is this more obvious than when George is injured in *Deathly Hallows* as they're trying to move Harry to the Burrow and they get attacked by Death Eaters. When George is brought in, bleeding from a lost ear, this is the first time in the entire series that we see Fred knocked down by fear: "For the first time since Harry had known him, Fred seemed to be lost for words" (74). But George knows what his role is—even then, missing an ear, he uses their shared sense of humor to comfort his twin. George's joke about feeling "holey" and "saintlike" brings color back to Fred's face, and Fred immediately teases him for the terrible joke (74-75)—their humor is their way of saying they love each other. This is their return to normalcy. They use humor to comfort each other, and it comforts everyone around them, too—the whole room feels warmer after their joking returns.

Later, when the trio is on the run searching for Horcruxes in *Deathly Hallows*, it's Fred's voice on the wireless radio that brings the trio back to life and brings them closer together, which gives them the strength to handle everything that comes right after—Malfoy Mansion, Dobby's death, and the battle. And Fred does not say something profound about bravery or about love or family; he jokes about Voldemort: "...he can move faster than Severus Snape confronted with shampoo" (444). When things are life and death, Fred knows how much we need a moment of levity—like a boggart, the more we can laugh at a thing, the less dangerous it becomes, and the less power it has over us.

Even in the day surrounding Fred's death, the absolute worst day, there are still reasons to laugh. In the middle of the Battle of Hogwarts, two of the school's iconic gargoyles are blasted apart, and they say to students and professors running by: "Oh, don't mind me...I'll just lie here and crumble" (620). We get to laugh with Harry as Ron and Hermione finally choose this moment, of all the other possible moments, to kiss. At the very end, Peeves still manages to get in one last rude song about Voldemort's defeat. And from the way we saw the twins comfort each other with their sense of humor throughout the series, we know that some part of their joy together lives on through George, even if it's now irrevocably changed. The Weasleys teach us that it's okay to laugh at the funerals in our lives—even though that person may be lost, we know that they existed and laughed, too.

On a broader scale, it can sometimes feel hard to laugh amid war and famine that exist somewhere else, or even right next door. But our laughter can be a way out, if only for a moment, of those dark spaces. Just like the trio as they fear for their lives after their escape from Gringotts on the back of a dragon in *Deathly Hallows*, we can still laugh at Ron's joke: "Well, I don't know how to break this to you...but I think they might have noticed we broke into Gringotts" (548). In that moment, their laughter is freedom from fear. Just like the best way to disarm a bully can be to laugh at them, laughter can give us a sense of power and control—rather than the darkness controlling us, our laughter is a way of fighting the darkness.

The lesson is not about humor at all, it turns out. The point is what the humor does: It brings people together. A sense of humor is not a deflection or avoidance—it is comfort; it is armor; it is a weapon against a life that too often tries to harm us. Like Fred and George's shared jokes, our laughter says that we understand each other, that we know we need a break, that we are armed together for the life ahead.

WINGARDIUM LEVIOSA: ON THE UNBEARABLE RIGHTNESS OF HERMIONE

When my sister and I were only four and six years old, my family needed more money, and so my stay-at-home mother went back to school to get a new Bachelor's degree, then a Master's, and then her doctorate. During the day, she ran a daycare center out of our house, tending to eight to ten toddlers all day, and at night she sat and flipped through a thick binder of notes at the kitchen table after we'd all gone to bed. From watching her, I absorbed what I thought I was supposed to do. I knew my job was, like hers, to work hard, and that that hard work would lead to something.

But in reality, it seemed, working hard wasn't always enough. As I got older and became a writer and professor, I felt the opposite. I watched as my male colleagues with the same experience as me got more classes and better schedules. I spoke up in meetings only to have my colleagues write notes with my ideas in them while they later completely forget that I'd been there at all. Was it me? Was it them? Was I a ghost? Over time, I started to think that I really must be a worse writer, a worse professor. I faded.

One night, I was playing a board game with some friends. The goal of the game was to lie and to hide your true identity as a traitor from the other players. I watched my wonderful nerdy male friends being happy with their wonderful nerdy selves. I often felt stupid playing games with them, even though I knew, deep down, that I wasn't stupid. But I wanted to win, so I played stupid. I played like I didn't understand the rules of the game. I asked questions that I already knew the answers to. I banged my hands on the table and pretended I was frustrated and that I didn't get it.

I won the game. For a few minutes, I felt amazing. I *wasn't* stupid. And better yet, I'd played them all. I could sit with them and feel just as smart as the rest of them. But soon, my poor-loser's joy at winning the game faded, too. This wasn't the joy of hard work paying off. I was 28 years old, but in order to look cool in front of the boys, my strategy was to play stupid. To make myself less. To make myself into exactly the stupid, useless woman I feared they thought I was.

Hogwarts, at times, can seem like a sexism-free paradise: Men and women live in dormitories together (though they're separated), women have clearly been in positions of power both at Hogwarts and in the Ministry of Magic for many thousands of years, and no one seems to care at all that the Quidditch teams are firmly coed. When Angelina Johnson is made Quidditch captain in *Order of the Phoenix*, Harry grins at her, and the team respects her leadership just as much as any of their male captains.

But, of course, no place is a sexism-free paradise, not even Hogwarts. As proof, we need to discuss the star of this chapter and of our hearts: Hermione. Hermione is both a representation of a stereotype, and an absolute ass-kicking breaker of stereotypes. Hermione can appear like a stereotypical woman when she's constantly bursting into tears or throwing her arms around someone. The men around her fall into stereotypical roles, too: Hermione is constantly told that she worries too much, or to calm down or lighten up, or that she's being uptight. The boys roll their eyes every time she cautions against something foolish that they're doing, claiming she's overprotective, she's shrill, she talks too much; she's just being Hermione—she's just being female.

But there's a reason Hermione is such a beloved character: She refuses the stereotype. She refuses to shut up and calm down. She might burst into tears, but she's also consistently the most prepared and most logical of the trio. Though she does occasionally lose her cool, ("But there's no wood!"[*Sorcerer's Stone*, 278]), she keeps it together more frequently than the boys do. While Harry and Ron often want to charge into the action, Hermione wants to stop and make a plan. In *Chamber of Secrets*, it's Hermione who comes up with the Polyjuice Potion plan to question Malfoy. In *Prisoner of Azkaban*, she is the only one who does research to help Hagrid make a plan for Buckbeak's trial; Harry and Ron quickly get distracted by Quidditch. In *Order of the Phoenix*, when Harry sees a vision of Sirius hurt at the Ministry, he wants to rush off as quickly as he can to help. But Hermione senses (correctly) that it might be a trap, and convinces Harry to make sure Sirius has actually left the house at Grimmauld Place before they go running to the Ministry. She even comes up with a plan to break into Umbridge's office. And when they're caught by Umbridge, it's Hermione who comes up with a fantastic lie to get Umbridge carried off by the centaurs, freeing the trio to follow their own plan. Harry, meanwhile, is useless—yelling and cursing and unable to think clearly. We don't blame Harry for his panicked terror and inability to think clearly when he fears Sirius is dying—most of us would likely react the same way. But in a moment where it counts, the one being the most rational, clearheaded, and clever is not a man, but Hermione.

And as they begin their search for the Horcruxes (the trio's darkest and most difficult undertaking), it's not Harry or Ron who prepare, but Hermione. And on the night that Death Eaters infiltrate Bill and Fleur's wedding, we discover that Hermione isn't just prepared for a brief overnight stay—she's prepared them for every possible contingency. She's packed books (and *The Tales of Beedle the Bard* come in handy); she's packed essence of dittany (which saves Ron's life after a Splinched Apparition); she's packed things a stereotypical mother might pack (extra robes, Muggle clothing, and Harry's own rucksack, with the photo album of his parents inside). And she's bewitched her small beaded bag to include their tent, and later, the necessary portrait of Phineas Nigellus. She doesn't just pack their bags for them; she saves their lives and she saves their sanity. As they head out on the run and try to live in the now-abandoned and desolate Grimmauld Place, Hermione's planning allows her to offer Harry the small comfort of his own toothbrush.

We may wonder if Hermione does these things *because* the boys don't do them, because women have been taught that we should take care of the cooking and packing and cleaning logistics. It's hard to say whether Hermione is just well-prepared, amazing Hermione, or if she (and the boys, too) are products of a culture of sexist expectations, forcing Hermione to act as project manager while Harry gets to be the idea man. But ultimately, it's Hermione's logistics, not Harry's ideas, that save them. When we arm ourselves for our own adventures, may we be as prepared to save our own lives as Hermione.

Hermione is always the most logical and the most prepared because she knows more than those people around her. She spends her life studying and learning, but never assumes that she's learned everything. Her quest for knowledge always keeps her looking forward; she's never satisfied with how much she knows. And because she knows so much, she's rightfully cautious. Almost every single time Hermione warns the trio of some potential danger, she's right. In *Sorcerer's Stone*, she's right that the duel with Malfoy is a setup to get Harry in trouble (159). In *Prisoner of Azkaban*, Hermione warns Harry not to go to Hogsmeade without his permission slip and later because of possible danger from Sirius Black, and of course Harry is seen by Malfoy and caught by Snape. Worse than Snape's interrogation, though, is Lupin's admonishment afterward about Harry's carelessness with his own safety: "Your parents gave their lives to keep you alive, Harry. A poor way to repay them—gambling their sacrifice for a bag of magic tricks" (290). Instead of listening to Hermione for this lesson, Harry must learn it the hard way. When Harry is gifted a mysterious Firebolt broomstick from a stranger, Hermione is worried that it's cursed or will otherwise try to hurt Harry, and insists they turn it in to Professor McGonagall to check. She suspects (again, correctly) it's from Sirius. Though they ultimately don't need to be worried about Sirius Black, her caution is to help protect her friend, even when she knows they'll be furious at her for taking the broomstick away. And Hermione's even skeptical of Scabbers, which, as it turns out, is a very wise fear.

Later, when the stakes become higher, Hermione is the only one in *Goblet of Fire* to worry about past deaths at the Triwizard Tournament. Everyone around her thinks she's too cautious, and that the tournament will just be a good bit of fun. But her worry foreshadows both Cedric's death and Voldemort's return. When the trio and Neville, Ginny, and Luna are at the Department of Mysteries in *Order of the Phoenix* (thanks to Hermione's planning), Hermione warns Harry not to touch the prophecy with his name on it (780). He does, and this is what calls the Death Eaters. Though others see Hermione as soft, her instincts are knife-sharp—she cuts through nonsense and sees the truth every time.

One of the rare things Hermione is wrong about is the Deathly Hallows. In her practical mind, she doesn't think they're real, and she doesn't think that Harry should pursue them. She's wrong; they are indeed real, but she's still right in her wariness. Though Harry needed to confront the Hallows in order to learn about wandlore and his own history as a descendent of the Peverells, the Hallows are still dangerous. Though it was necessary to learn about their history, perhaps it was Hermione's caution that kept Harry from being swept up and consumed by the Hallows the same way Dumbledore was. He's able to wield their power without succumbing to them. Harry eventually comes to the same conclusion that Hermione came to hundreds of pages earlier: He should continue his quest to destroy Horcruxes, and not start a new one to find the Hallows. Yet again, Hermione's caution is warranted.

In addition to her book smarts, Hermione also displays a kind of emotional intelligence that Harry and Ron do not. When Harry gets his first girlfriend, Hermione has to explain to Harry that Cho Chang might be feeling conflicted about her feelings for Harry and his proximity to Cedric's death. She senses Sirius's confusing relationship with Harry, who reminds him of his long-lost friend: "But I sometimes think Ron's mum's right, and Sirius gets confused about whether you're you or your father, Harry" (*Order of the Phoenix,* 159). Harry's immediately furious, thinking Hermione's saying Sirius is insane. She shrugs, and says, "No, I just think he's been very lonely for a long time" (159). She knows that Harry will respond badly to being kept in the dark the summer before the Order of the Phoenix is formed. She knows he will respond badly to the plan to disguise others in his image in order to move him from the Dursleys in *Deathly Hallows.* She knows when all isn't right between Tonks and Lupin. Her emotional intelligence allows her to see the people around her more clearly, and gives her insight into their motivation. Perhaps we can move through the world as competently as Hermione if we can learn to understand others as well as she does.

But Hermione is never taken seriously. She's told to stop worrying. In *Chamber of Secrets,* Hermione is symbolically silenced the way she's silenced throughout the series—she has the secret to the mystery clutched in her fist, but she's unconscious, and cannot tell anyone. Would it have mattered, though? She's hardly ever listened to while she's conscious, despite how often the boys discover that she was right all along. And the treatment of Ginny in *Chamber of Secrets* is even worse—even though the entire story revolves around her, her behavior is dismissed as being the result of "girl stuff," as her simply having a crush, and no one bothers to talk to her more. Yet Harry's victory over Tom Riddle in *Chamber of Secrets* is mostly thanks to Hermione. She manages to lend her brain even while she's unconscious.

Not only is Hermione never seen as an authority, but she's also rarely appreciated. The boys see her as a nag more often than anything else. As the books progress, the boys do occasionally thank Hermione, but they still leave the planning work to her, and they still see her as a meddling worrywart. Even though her caution is often taken to protect Harry and Ron, they see her and Molly Weasley the same way—as women who do what they're supposed to do: wash their socks, cook their dinner, share homework with them, and then go away. The boys have chances to learn that they should take Hermione seriously, but they don't. In *Prisoner of Azkaban*, when the boys are angry at Hermione for reporting the mysterious Firebolt and for being unable to control her cat Crookshanks around Ron's rat Scabbers, Hagrid tells Harry and Ron, "I thought you two'd value yer friend more'n broomsticks or rats. Tha's all" (274). And even then, Ron, rather than listening, stays angry about Crookshanks's behavior.

Is it any wonder that Hermione snaps and slaps Malfoy after he calls Hagrid pathetic? Is it any wonder that, after a lifetime of worrying about and caring for people, Molly Weasley gets the chance to take action for Ginny, and screams, "Not my daughter, you bitch!" (*Deathly Hallows,* 736) at Bellatrix Lestrange in that final battle, right before killing her? In the final moments of the last big battle, the clamor falls away to watch Molly Weasley and Bellatrix battle each other, all eyes finally on the caretaker and force who's long since deserved their gaze. We love her all-caps scream because this is, at last, Molly's glorious moment: Here she is both a housewife and a powerful witch, capable of great power and great love at once.

I admit I feel conflicted and disappointed that Hermione marries Ron. Even J. K. Rowling has admitted that, after some distance, she questions her choice to marry them. Ron is only kind to Hermione at the very end (and only because *Twelve Fail-Safe Ways to Charm Witches* tells him to be). He only shows interest in house-elves (one of Hermione's main interests) at the finale. I'm not sure that Ron has earned Hermione's love, or that he'll appreciate her going forward. Additionally, despite the many times that Hermione is told she's the smartest witch of her year, or a good girl, or how often Harry and Ron tell her that she's a lifesaver for helping with their homework, at the end of the series it's Harry who gets credit for defeating Voldemort. History will remember Harry, but not Hermione. At the end of the series, even adult Harry is still recognized on Platform 9¾. Hermione is just someone's wife.

In spite of this inherent unfairness, perhaps the greatest thing about Hermione is the fact that she stays completely herself. Despite the fact that she's continually mocked and disrespected and ignored, she never changes who she is. She hardly ever doubts herself. She stands by her values and never stops working hard. She stays clever; she stays kind. And she always promotes what is right, even if it's something as small as the proper pronunciation of *Wingardium Leviosa*.

And even if they don't appreciate it, she will continue to protect the people she loves. In *Prisoner of Azkaban*, Hermione takes her fears about the mysterious Firebolt broomstick delivered to Harry to McGonagall (a woman who also deserves her own chapter), who takes the broomstick away. Ron and Harry are furious with Hermione, but though "she was still pink in the face, [she] stood up and faced Ron defiantly" (232). She refuses to let the bastards grind her down.

Even if she were playing a game, Hermione would never play dumb. From Hermione, we can learn to hold onto who we are to keep from drowning in what we think we should be. From Hermione, we can remind ourselves that we need to listen to women. We need to believe them when they say they have been hurt, and we need to listen when they say we could be hurt, too. We need to trust that women are smart and capable. We need to believe ourselves smart and capable. Thank god for the hard-working women in our lives. Thank god for Hermione. Thank god for insufferable know-it-alls.

PETRIFICUS TOTALUS: ON BRAVERY

One afternoon, standing in the hallway of the school where I teach, I was a coward. One of my students stood there talking to a former student. The former student did not seem to recognize me. He stood asking my other student question after question. She responded in monosyllables. He kept talking. She smiled in the way all women have learned—to appease someone without trying to encourage them, to keep them from getting upset. She made occasional eye contact with him, but otherwise, she tried to look elsewhere. She turned just a little bit so that she was not directly facing him. He continued talking, despite her obvious cues that she was trying to leave. I caught her eye and gave her a sympathetic smile. That's it. I went inside my classroom. I left.

As professor to both of them, I was in a position of power and I failed to intervene. The student was not in danger, of course, but every bit of her body language suggested she was trapped somewhere she did not want to be. All it would have taken was for me to step in and say hello, and ask if she had a minute to speak to me. She would've been free to decline. Why didn't I? Even as a professor, I'd gotten stuck in that old, shy habit of not wanting to bother anyone. I justified it to myself—she didn't need my help, anyway. I didn't want to be too pushy. But these are justifications for only one version of this story. What if she did need help? What then?

When the time comes for us to be bold, we sometimes shrink. Being bold means being visible, vulnerable. It is easier to let ourselves be carried than to carry others.

Perhaps the biggest lesson we can learn from the *Harry Potter* series is how to be brave. We learn this lesson from observing characters responding to fear. We see fear in the Dursleys: their fear of Hagrid, of Hogwarts, of magic, of Sirius, and of anything out of the ordinary. We see fear in Fudge and in the wizarding community's avoidance of facing Voldemort's return. We see fear in Dumbledore's tendency to avoid telling the whole truth. We see fear in Ron and in Lupin as they try to face difficulty. We see fear in the violence of the Death Eaters and Voldemort. And we see fear in Harry every time someone he loves is threatened and he must face the unexpected. But each time, he does as Emily Dickinson says: "If your nerve deny you / go above your nerve."[5] Bravery is the rope that each character holds in order to find their way back to each other and back to themselves.

5   Emily Dickinson, "292," *The Complete Poems of Emily Dickinson*, edited by Thomas H. Johnson, New York: Little Brown, 1960, 136.

This chapter is named for Neville, who gets his first taste of bravery when, in *Sorcerer's Stone*, he tries to keep the trio from leaving the common room after hours and losing Gryffindor more points. Taking the trio's own advice to stick up for himself, he even puts up his fists. To stop him, Hermione miserably casts *Petrificus Totalus*, binding Neville. Though you could read *Petrificus Totalus* as a metaphor for the kind of paralysis fear gives you, I'd rather read it as foreshadowing—this is just a small version of Neville's willingness to put himself in front of a wand for a bigger cause. His bravery only grows.

We see bravery in Harry—occasionally to the point of stupidity, but his bravery is often immensely selfless. We see bravery in Hagrid and Hermione's kindness, and in Hermione's willingness to stand up for herself and for others. We see bravery in Lupin and in Fred and George, for defying the expectations set for them. And we see bravery in Snape—laboring in a life that brings him no joy, in service to a love that will never be requited, but doing the work because the work feels worth it just the same.

From Harry, Snape, and Dumbledore, we can learn the bravery of facing our demons, the things we've done that haunt us. Even as late as *Deathly Hallows*, Harry is forced to confront his own sense of inadequacy. He doubts his ability to be a leader. He worries his magic is not enough. He worries that his anger and impulsiveness and tendency to want revenge has lead him into all the wrong decisions. He worries, more than anything, that he is letting everyone down. Similarly, Snape spends his whole life confronting one mistake that he made. Dumbledore, too, must reexamine the racist choices he made when he was young, how they affected Grindelwald and his family, and reckon with the ways they reflect forward into the present. But reckoning with these inadequacies is brave—it makes Harry, Dumbledore, and Snape better. The characters who aren't willing face their own faults (Voldemort, Karkaroff, Pettigrew, among others) keep blindly retracing the old, worn paths within themselves, and eventually they wear themselves down to nothing, and they get lost. Our ability to face our own faults is our ability to understand the places we must not go, and it brightens the paths we might not have seen otherwise.

From the series, we can also learn the bravery required to face our own worst feelings. Out of all the characters in the books, Harry struggles the most with his feelings, probably because growing up with the Dursleys, his feelings were completely ignored. He is an amplified version of all of us, cycling between rage and sadness and shame and joy and back again like spring thunderstorms. Snape, while giving Harry Occlumency lessons to help him close his mind to Voldemort, serves as the voice for shutting feelings down: "...Fools who wear their hearts proudly on their sleeves, who cannot control their emotions, who wallow in sad memories and allow themselves to be provoked this easily—weak people, in other words—they stand no chance against his powers!" (*Order of the Phoenix,* 536).

Snape is both right and wrong. Harry's ability to feel is both a weakness and a strength. He's made to feel terrible pain, and his desire for revenge is manipulated by Voldemort. But his ability to feel pain is what saves him. When Harry is feeling the immense grief of losing Sirius, Dumbledore says, "suffering like this proves you are still a man!... This pain is part of being human" (824). But Voldemort can no longer feel pain like Harry's, and thus has made himself less of a human. In

Order of the Phoenix, while Voldemort is possessing Harry, Harry's wish to see Sirius again is so strong that Voldemort's soul is unable to handle it, and this love drives Voldemort out. And later, in *Deathly Hallows*, Harry's grief for Dobby is what allows him to finally, at last, block Voldemort's thoughts from his brain.

He may not realize it, but Snape's speech about "fools who wear their hearts proudly on their sleeves" equally applies to his own life and his fear of finding the bravery required to face his own heartbreak (*Order of the Phoenix*, 473). Though Snape hides his true love and grief for Lily from all around him out of fear of appearing foolish, the fact is that Snape's life is built upon sad memories and emotion. All of his adult choices, including the many times he saves Harry's life, are the result of what Dumbledore calls "the best" part of Snape—the love and the grief and anger he can't openly face (*Deathly Hallows*, 679). Like Harry, Snape's greatest love is also his greatest strength. But what might Snape's life have been like if he'd had the bravery to truly face his emotions? Would he have been able to build a real relationship with Harry, who held a shred of Lily Potter, or with anyone at all? Would his life have held just a bit less darkness? Just as Hagrid is willing to carry both the bodies of Dumbledore and Harry, facing our difficult feelings allows us to face ourselves and our deepest loves. The range of our emotions, if we are brave enough to feel them all, is what allows us to experience the world in all its bright and painful colors.

From Fred, George, Luna, Professor McGonagall, and Hermione (and a few other members of Dumbledore's Army, too), may we learn the bravery to stand alone. It's easier to slip into the crowd, hope no one notices you, and disappear. Hermione sticks up for the house-elves when no one else will, no matter how much she's teased about it. When Professor Trelawney is cruelly sacked by Umbridge, McGonagall steps away from the crowd watching her humiliation to comfort her. This action gives Professors Sprout and Flitwick courage to step out, too, and help Trelawney upstairs.

Luna's bravery also emboldens others to break free of the crowd. When no one believes Harry's story that Voldemort has returned, Luna is unafraid to say publicly that she supports Harry (and later, Ernie Macmillan becomes fearless, too, and says the same). Sometimes the stakes feel highest when we're around our peers, and we'd rather blend in than stand out and embarrass ourselves. But Luna's commitment to the truth is stronger than her own ego. And when Voldemort takes over, Fred and George create the radio show *Potterwatch*. At a time when disappearing would be the easiest, they refuse. And during the reign of the Death Eaters at Hogwarts, Neville's beaten up by the Carrows; Terry Boot yells about the trio's dragon escape from Gringotts in the Great Hall (even though it means punishment), and even Michael Corner risks torture when he frees an imprisoned first-year. As Neville says, "...it helps when people stand up to them, it gives everyone hope" (*Deathly Hallows*, 574).

And from Harry and from Dumbledore, may we learn the bravery it takes to be merciful. Harry lets Peter Pettigrew go. Even when Pettigrew's silver hand remembers this act of mercy and turns upon its owner, both Harry and Ron show Pettigrew mercy a second time, and try to save him from himself. Harry shows mercy each time he uses *Expelliarmus* instead of the Unforgivable Curses. When Neville is being tortured in the Department of Mysteries as bait, Harry immediately gives up the prophecy. In that moment, the mercy to save his friend is far more important than the prophecy. And Dumbledore shows mercy to Draco Malfoy, in the last moments of Dumbledore's life. Dumbledore organizes his own death with Snape to give a 17-year-old the mercy of a life unblemished by murder. From this, we learn that we can all take the small chances for mercy in our own lives. It is brave to be merciful to someone who terrifies you or who hurt you because they could fail to live up to your mercy. But mercy also gives others a chance to do better.

The twin of this mercy is believing the best of people, like Dumbledore and Hermione do. Like giving mercy, believing the best of people is a kind of blind trust—trust without proof. We all know that people will let us down, so believing in them still is a kind of bravery. Hermione believes the best in Harry, even when he doesn't live up to her belief. This belief and their friendship is what saves them both—they need each other's beliefs in their best selves in order to defeat Voldemort. Hermione believes the best in Dumbledore—believes in *his* belief in Snape, believes in him even when Harry questions Dumbledore's past. Snape himself, a skeptic, says that Dumbledore's greatest weakness is that "he has to believe the best of people" (*Half-Blood Prince,* 31). And though Dumbledore is often let down by others' behavior, we know that Snape is wrong: Dumbledore's "weakness" allows him to trust Snape. His belief in the best in Snape is a bravery that fulfills Snape's greatest desire: to absolve him of the guilt of Lily Potter's death, and to keep her son safe.

Part of believing the best in others is being brave enough to empathize with what they must be feeling, whether we can really understand it or not. Hermione often works hard to empathize with Harry (while Ron sometimes struggles), even when she doesn't understand him. Dumbledore feels deeply for Harry—after Sirius's death, Dumbledore allows Harry to rage at him because he understands the tumble of guilt and pain. Dumbledore has empathy because he has felt that guilt and pain himself; he thinks he might be guilty of his own sister's death. Meanwhile, Voldemort has lost the ability to feel empathy for others, and so he's lost a bit of his humanity. We believe the best in others because they could be us, or we could be them. Feeling empathy for others, the way Harry can see inside Voldemort's head, is a kind of bravery—it forces us to see the whole human spectrum, no matter how terrible or how beautiful.

May we learn from the many mothers in the series the bravery of sacrifice. Lily Potter, Barty Crouch Jr.'s mother, Molly Weasley, and Tonks all sacrifice themselves, in one way or another, for their children to have better lives. Everything Molly Weasley does is for someone other than herself. But this lesson of sacrifice doesn't only come from mothers or parents: Lupin, Dumbledore, Snape, and of course, Harry, all can teach us about sacrifice. Most of these people sacrifice their lives for those they love. Though most of us will never face the kind of sacrifice most of these characters encounter, launching themselves in front of a wand to save someone they love, we can learn from this kind of bravery. While Voldemort lives his life for his own immortality, the others live for their communities and families. As Lupin says of his son Teddy, "...he will know why I died and I hope he will understand. I was trying to make a world in which he could live a happier life" (*Deathly Hallows*, 700). This kind of bravery means understanding the world through a broader lens than your own two eyes can provide. The point is not for us to walk into the woods like Harry, giving up our own lives for others. Instead, the point is that we are able to be brave for someone besides ourselves.

At the same time, from Arthur Weasley, from Hermione, and even from Percy, may we learn the bravery of being absolutely ourselves. Despite cruel teasing, Arthur never gives up his nerdy interest in Muggle technology. Though Percy does lose his way, he stays true to his rule-following, perfect-prefect self. Hermione, as we've seen, almost never stops believing in herself.

Perhaps the best example of the bravery in being yourself is Luna Lovegood. Luna, who wears huge lion hats and radish earrings. Luna, who isn't bothered when others tease her about Nargles or steal her things. Despite the many things that Luna has to face in her life, she is the least troubled of anyone. She wears her own skin the way the rest of us might wear our best dress. Even when she's been trapped in the basement dungeon at Malfoy Manor, Luna is still her kind, strange, thoughtful self. Her bravery is one that refuses to let the world change her.

And most of all, may we learn to be brave enough to trust others, and to hope. Harry (and Dumbledore, too) is afraid to trust others because he would rather take things on alone. But because we are vulnerable when we trust others, trust is a form of bravery. Hope is a form of bravery. In the end, Harry is at his best when he is willing to trust his friends, to trust

Dumbledore, and to take a bit of the pressure off himself. And his friends' trust in Harry is their own form of bravery—they cannot know if he will prevail (and in fact, he doesn't even know), but they do best when they trust in each other.

May we all be as brave as Harry, about to put on the Sorting Hats and destroy the Horcruxes we might face. May we be as brave as Neville, with our wands pointed at those who might harm us, even if they are our friends. May we be worth 12 of the Malfoys in our own lives. May we distrust fate and trust our own selves a little more. May we be as selfless as Hermione and as Snape, and be willing to sacrifice parts of ourselves for those who need our protection. May we always have power like Molly Weasley, and joy like Arthur and Fred and George. May we be like Ron, and brave enough to change our minds and to say we are sorry. May we be as sure as Luna that the things we've lost will return to us in some form or another. And even when the world feels like it's ending, may we have friends and loves that feel like magic.

ACKNOWLEDGMENTS

⚡⚡⚡

I've spent a lot of time thinking about the incredible magic that meant that I got to write this, my first book. Without the absolute lucky abundance of support around me, the book would never have happened. Thank you, thank you, thank you.

Thank you first to my family, especially my sister Beth (who read *Sorcerer's Stone* first and told me I should really check out this new book), for being my first Hogwarts House. Thank you for your hours spent reading with me, Amanda, Megan, Jessie, Matt, Grace, Kate, and Caroline. And thank you to my parents for your endless support and patience, even when I insisted on reading at the dinner table.

Thank you to my friends who were always willing to have long conversations with me about wandlore and house-elf rights (while others got bored and walked away), especially Alisa, Angela, Jo, Ashley, Anna, Emily, Krista, Sara, Stephanie, Ian, Alex, and Renee, and to all of you who were willing to indulge my requests for *Harry Potter* movie marathons, to go with me to midnight showings, and who remembered to ask how the book was going (especially you, Sunni), or offered to bring me coffee, booze, or butterbeer.

Thank you to Marcia Aldrich, Marilyn Abildskov, and Wesley Gibson for your mentorship, and to my dear MFA classmates. I would not be who I am without you. Wesley, I wish you were here to tease me about this book.

Thank you to all the people who were brave enough to lend me their stories for this book—my parents, my sister, my grandpa Roger, my Busia, Alisa, Sunni, Lindsey, Greta, my Aunt Pam, and Pamela Wall.

Thank you to KMA Sullivan and the YesYes Books crew for their support and constant, necessary cheerleading while I neglected them in order to write this.

Thank you to Kat Finch, for your kind gesture of selflessness, and to the 3-4-5, and to the Binders—without you, this book wouldn't exist.

Thank you to Michele Brusseau for her *Harry Potter* class that I somehow lucked into taking as a graduate student. Many of my ideas for this book took shape there, though I didn't even know it at the time.

Thank you Ulysses Press for choosing me for this project. Specifically, thanks to editors Shayna Keyles and Bridget Thoreson and publicist Molly Conway, who believed in this book from the beginning, and who helped make it a fully formed Patronus, instead of just the wisps of smoke from which it began.

Thank you to Vanessa Zoltan and Casper ter Kuile of the *Harry Potter and the Sacred Text* podcast, whose thoughtful discussions inspired me throughout this book, and who gave me the incredible gift of reading *Harry Potter* as if it's sacred (which, of course, it is). And thank you to my Bay Area Writing Project friend Eva for introducing the podcast to me (and to my other teacher-friend-colleagues Scott and Chris for always being willing to analyze *Harry Potter* with me).

Thank you to *shinyswablu*, a random stranger on the Internet who made the Hufflepuff Commonroom ambient noise mix on Ambientmixer.com. I wrote most of this book listening to it.

Thank you to J. K. Rowling for giving me one of the greatest loves of my life.

Thank you to my students for giving me another. Thank you too, students, for your patience with my slow grading while I wrote this book, and for promising to buy it. Thank you to all of you for your bravery and your laughter. You make me believe in magic every single day.

Thank you to *you*, whom I shouldn't have forgotten. Please forgive me.

And thank you to my husband Charlie, who's told me for years that I should write a *Harry Potter* book. I should have listened much sooner. Lots of people dislike the epilogue to *Deathly Hallows* because they say no one ends up with their high school sweetheart. But I ended up with mine. Thank you for understanding my tears on the Hogwarts Express, for every dinner you cooked, and for every hour you didn't mind that I spent huddled over my computer. I still don't believe in fate, Charlie, but I believe in you.